New Frontiers in Sensory Integration

Limbic Stimulation, Authentic Relationship and a Multi-Disciplinary Treatment Design

By Stephanie Mines, Ph.D.

NEW FORUMS PRESS INC.

Published in the United States of America
by New Forums Press, Inc. 1018 S. Lewis St.
Stillwater, OK 74074
www.newforums.com

Copyright © 2014 by New Forums Press, Inc.

All rights reserved. No part of this publication may be reproduced or transmitted in any form or by any means, electronic or mechanical, including photocopy, or any information storage or retrieval system, without permission in writing from the publisher.

Library of Congress Cataloging-in-Publication Data Pending

This book may be ordered in bulk quantities at discount from New Forums Press, Inc., P.O. Box 876, Stillwater, OK 74076 [Federal I.D. No. 73 1123239]. Printed in the United States of America.

Illustrations by Patricia Raine, Doya Nardin and Mara Giulini

ISBN 10: 1-58107-265-1
ISBN 13: 978-1-58107-265-5

Contents

Dedication ---iv

Acknowledgments --v

Note to Readers of This Book on the Use
of the Term: Neurodiversity --- vii

Preface---ix

Foreword---xi

Introduction: *A Remarkable Case Study*---------------------------------- xiii

PART ONE: Awareness ---1

CHAPTER ONE: *Assessing Sensory Systems:*
A Primer for the Diagnostic Journey------------------------------------3

CHAPTER TWO: *How to Use Your Brain as an*
Anchor for a Child with Sensory Needs --------------------------------- 29

CHAPTER THREE: *The Art of Limbic Stimulation*
for Motivation and Connection--- 43

CHAPTER FOUR: *The Road to Damascus: Changing*
Perceptions of Sensory Challenge ------------------------------------- 59

PART TWO: Embodiment --- 72

CHAPTER FIVE: *Applied Touch Treatments*------------------------------- 75

CHAPTER SIX: *The Dancing Brain: Using*
the Arts for Brain Resiliency---101

CHAPTER SEVEN: *Cultivating Niche Construction*
for Sensory Integration---127

CHAPTER EIGHT: *The Triumphant Children and*
Their Families: The Path from Diagnosis to Advocacy-----------------159

End Notes ---181

Bibliography---189

References --195

About the Author---201

Dedication

This book is dedicated to all children who call to us to hear their inner song and see their essence and to the parents who advocate for them and evolve themselves as they parent. I also dedicate this book to my own grandchildren, Simone and Sophia, and to my daughters Rachel and Sierra.

Finally, this book lovingly memorializes a profound mentor, Donita Petersen, PT, who died in March, 2013. She lives on in all those who she touched with her skill and faith.

Acknowledgements

I am indebted to an exceptional group of Physical and Occupational Therapists who steered me in the direction of pediatrics. Their faith in the value of my treatment formula, the TARA Approach, for children with special needs continues to fuel my creativity. I am inspired by their capacity to underscore health and potential by truly seeing it and supporting it with specific interventions, based on each individual child they touch. They do not relate primarily to dysfunction or symptoms. Rather they orient themselves towards the human beings they encounter and apply the highly developed skills they consistently cultivate and amplify. I respect their capacities enormously and thus was honored when they chose to become my students and incorporate the TARA Approach into their own practices. In fact it seems odd to think of them as my students as I considered them my mentors.

I am delighted to have this opportunity to express my gratitude to Kay Davis, PT, Margo Hayes, PT, Holly Jones, PT, Dianna Persun, OT, Donita Petersen, PT, Amy Reid, PT, and Micah Sale, PT. Without them this book would not exist.

Stephanie Mines, Ph.D.

Stephanie Mines, Ph.D.

Note to Readers of This Book on the Use of the Term: Neurodiversity

"Each individual brain is like a unique rainforest, teeming with growth, decay, competition, diversity and selection."
❖ Gerald Edelman (Cornwell 2007)

The coining, understanding and use of the word "neurodiversity" is a gateway. It opens to allow us to see both the landscape from which we are departing and the one ahead. It is an evolutionary word marking a turning point in how we educate about and comprehend development. The word neurodiversity is also a mirror that reflects how we are adapting to a broad spectrum of influences that shape our learning and relationships with one another. Neurodiversity is not a word about autism alone. It is a word that embraces all neurological uniqueness, all rhythms of neurodevelopment and all the forms by which humans can express themselves and contribute to their world.

I use the word neurodiversity throughout this book. The word is only a little more than a decade old. It refers to the proven fact that no two brains are alike. It also refers to the new and proliferating research that redefines the brain with an emphasis on its resiliency, its responsiveness, its bounty of complex connections, and its fluidity. We have moved out of the conceptualization of the brain as machinery and into the truer depiction of it as mobile and vital. In this book I refer to the playground quality of the brain with neural connections occurring continuously in response to learning.

Children and youth who have been labeled with autism, learning challenges or sensory processing difficulties may prefer to use the word neurodiverse for themselves. This does not mean that they are without a need for services. From their perspective using the word neurodiverse may reduce stigma. When we use language to exclude we dampen potential. Inclusion promotes limbic stimulation.

I also use words like "sensory needs" and "learning challenged" and "autism spectrum" because these are familiar. We are transitioning into terminology like "neurodiverse" and I respect the transition.

Preface
A Personal Statement from the Author

Writing this book has opened my eyes to personal as well as intellectual, theoretical and professional understanding. Just as I advocate for tolerance and creativity in welcoming human diversity so have I been awakened to more tolerance for myself as a neurodiverse individual. I have seen, in the light of my heightened perception of what neurodiversity is and what it means for us culturally, that the brain struggles under the weight of rejection, including auto-rejection. The need to self-validate and nourish one's neurodiversity is just as significant as making that request of others.

In this book I promote ways to witness and mentor all children who are wonderfully neurodiverse. I have fallen in love with the word and embrace it as a way out of the trap of otherness and assumptions that hide the truth of differentiated individuality. I also embrace the word as a new dimension of my relationship with myself. I think many adults who read this book may come to a similar discovery. This will go a long way towards spreading the message of tolerance and inclusion that I intend as an outcome not just of reading this book but of directly using the tools and ideas presented here.

Foreword

There have been precious moments, within my 38 years in the field of special education, when I have met individuals that "see" children with significant disabilities in a holistic way. It is more the norm for these children to be described by their deficits than their abilities, and the underpinnings of a developmental perspective in terms of their emotions and sensory profile is often neglected in exchange for a more behavioral approach.

My background is in Autism, with a specialty in Rett Syndrome, and while reading *New Frontiers in Sensory Integration,* I felt Stephanie's kinship on each page. If you were watching me read, you would have seen my head nodding emphatically while writing in the margins, as Stephanie's insights into Rett Syndrome mirrored things I have said and taught to others with the added treasure of the specifics of a neurological and sensory understanding that I knew at a "gut level" but didn't have the technical framework for. For the last 24 years, I have helped countless girls and women with Rett Syndrome learn to communicate, read and write. This success is with a population that was thought to be severely cognitively impaired with little hope for progress over time. I have always felt my job was to help these girls emerge more than teach them discreet skills – Stephanie's book would support that.

In a world, looking for "quick fixes" or "low-ball expectations" for our most neurologically diverse individuals, I was most struck by her discussion of being present and also how her understanding of the sensory system grounds what she does to open doors for those who cannot open them on their own. This book is significant for teachers, parents, friends and all those working with, living with and loving individuals whose "neurodiversity" can truly be a beginning and not an end.

Susan Norwell, Educational Specialist
Co-founder, www. Rett-U.org

Stephanie Mines, Ph.D.

Introduction
A Remarkable Case Study

This book focuses on providing support for children with autism and sensory needs though the resources contained here can be used effectively for all children. The causes behind what we call Sensory Processing Disorders remain unknown despite ongoing research. This is because causation is likely a mixed bag of genetic, epigenetic, environmental, neurodevelopmental and cultural factors. The important question that this book addresses is what we as parents, therapists, educators and care-providers can do about this growing epidemic in an empowered and sustainable way, no matter the causation.

My experiences with Sophie, who has been diagnosed with Rett Syndrome, a neurodevelopmental dysfunction on the autism spectrum, offer a model of what is possible even when sensory struggles are extreme. When I first met Sophie all I saw were her eyes. I did not notice her hands that were curved and nestled against each other like two agitated birds. Now, after years of treating Sophie I realize that by falling into compassion and attunement with her I likely provide the most advanced and meaningful service possible. My work with her combined with her mother's advocacy and follow-through has allowed her to enter adolescence without a wheelchair, create art, communicate with others and be dynamically interactive and expressive. This far exceeds the standard prognosis for this condition. Today Sophie is flourishing as a teenager in high school, participating in activities and making friends.

Sophie's mother comments that she learns about how to interact with Sophie by observing us together. This relationship is a reciprocal exchange that honors Sophie's intelligence. The diverse interventions I employ combine with our interactions to create a design that significantly augments current clinical applications for autism and sensory dysfunction. It is my template for limbic stimulation.

Rett Syndrome was identified by Dr. Andreas Rett, an Austrian physician who first described it in a journal article in 1966. A second article about the disorder published in 1983 led to its official recognition. The inability to plan and subsequently perform motor functions is perhaps the most severely disabling feature of Rett Syndrome which is caused by mutations in the MECP2 gene, found on the X chromosome. The MECP2 gene contains instructions for the synthesis of a binding protein that acts as a biochemical switch telling other genes when to turn off and stop producing their own unique proteins. Rett Syndrome affects girls almost exclusively. The genetic mutations appear random. It is believed that the mutation occurs during spermatogenesis. Signs of Rett's show up when the child is between six to eighteen months old. Vague symptoms gain a progressive intensity; particularly the hand wringing or hand clapping that is the tell-tale indicator.

Sophie's range of expression may be masked to the casual observer but an attentive person notices the lifting of an eyebrow, the darting of her tongue, the suggestion of meaning in sounds that verge on words and sometimes become them. These are just some of Sophie's many gestures towards participation and inclusion. From my observations Sophie is almost always articulating feeling.

Sophie and I interact in a multitude of ways, and we take advantage of opportunities to clarify and verify our understandings of each other. I dialogue with Sophie about what I am going to do and gain her consent, or accept her choice to change the course of treatment or end a session. She tells me a great deal by turning one way or the other on the treatment table, or by the softening or tightening of her musculature. Since Sophie began to actively use an eye gaze communication device that we call her "talker," she lets me know what kind of treatment she wants to receive and when.

Sophie is on the verge of womanhood. Her mother is her best friend and ally. She and I have identified fourteen major changes in Sophie since we began our therapeutic relationship. These are:

1. Enhanced fine motor skills, including reaching for what she wants like food, a toy or clothing, and bringing it to herself and then using it. Most recently this also includes reaching for an icon on her eye gaze device or a computer screen.
2. Increased and more diverse facial movement like nose wrinkling to express distaste, various kinds of smiles reflecting interpersonal responses, expressions of curiosity, sadness and mirth such as laughing at jokes, or directing her eyes to what she wants to communicate about. Her self-initiated practice of directing her eyes to what she is interested in or wants to discuss is reaping considerable benefit in the use of her eye gaze device for communication.
3. More social engagement, particularly reaching out to others who are new in her world and interacting with them appropriately. Sophie develops relationships. These were primarily with adults but now as an adolescent her relationships are maturing to include more peers.
4. Increased direct and self-initiated expression through gestures, sounds, word articulation or the use of augmented communication devices. Sophie clearly communicates when she wants to start, stop or change activities, such as therapy.
5. Periods of "quiet hands" and alternate uses of her hands in contrast to the singular and obsessive hand-clapping or hand-wringing that is the hallmark of Rett Syndrome.
6. Increased and more consistent muscular release, meaning that muscles let go of tension and soften. Rigidity or spasticity is common with Rett Syndrome. For this reason releases of muscle tension indicate a significant somatic shift. As Sophie has grown and matured muscular release can be voluntary and occurs upon request.
7. Softening of her respiratory diaphragm, another hallmark area of tightness for girls with Rett Syndrome. Since we began our relationship Sophie has avoided almost entirely all the respiratory ailments that had afflicted her previously. Respiratory problems are typical with Rett Syndrome.
8. Regularity of breathing patterns including consistently deeper respiration. This means that her habit of holding her breath, common in Rett Syndrome, has virtually disappeared.

9. More displays of joy, including appreciating art, theater, and music. Sophie indicates pleasure whenever she is understood correctly, which is clearly a source of delight for her. As a teenager Sophie expresses pleasure in the things that are typical for her age like clothing and social exchanges.
10. Ability to sustain attention in holding onto objects and using them is increased in both duration and frequency. This was also noted by Sophie's equine therapist who observed Sophie holding on to the bar while riding for longer periods of time. Sophie can also push a stroller or shopping cart and walk on a treadmill for as long as twenty minutes now. This means there is no hand-clapping during this period.
11. Less shyness or holding back when introduced to new people, including her peers. Her increased confidence is in marked contrast to previous anxiety about meeting people and has been noted by others such as support group parents and neighbors.
12. Sophie now readily moves towards a goal by walking steadily in the direction of what she wants with a balanced stride. This is contrasted with her previous asymmetrical, wobbly gait. Sophie retrieves desired objects and walks with them deliberately. Holding and carrying of objects requires cessation of hand-wringing or clapping.
13. Decreased jaw clenching or teeth grinding. This is another Rett characteristic which is common and has now decreased for Sophie by more than 60%.
14. There have and continue to be marked changes in the rhythms and qualities of Sophie's hand-clapping or hand-wringing. Especially after receiving applied touch treatments Sophie's hands move more slowly. Her fingers spread open rather than clenching into fists. She strokes the fingers of her opposite hand rather than clapping with intensity. There is overall less force in the hand-clapping and this is mirrored by a softening in her face and particularly in her jaw. Sophie uses her hands voluntarily more often in gestures that are expressive and communicate her needs.

The Interventions

These fourteen indicators of growth and improvement are a direct response to interventions I introduced into Sophie's life. These interventions are:

- ***Applied Touch***: I utilize an ancient Japanese meridian or acu-touch system that I have studied for over thirty years called Jin Shin. It employs touch on specific areas that stimulate what is known in Oriental medicine as the extraordinary meridians or eight reservoirs of energy. Like the ordinary meridians, the extraordinary meridians (also called the Rivers of Splendor) respond by awakening an innate healing response. They do this best with repeated contact. Pressure is not necessary but can be used if the child prefers it as some children with sensory needs do. Two areas on connective tissue are always held in concert. This system can be learned by parents and repeated at home. This is one of its stellar attractions.

    The applied touch system I use was rediscovered from antiquity in Japan by a man named Jiro Murai. He taught the system to my teacher, Mary Iino who brought it to the United States after she married an American and became Mary Iino Burmeister. I met Mary in California in 1975 and studied prodigiously with her until she died in 2008. After completing a doctoral program that focused on the treatment of head injury and neurodiversity I integrated what I had learned from Mary into my approach to nervous system reorganization. Successful clinical trials in the treatment of aphasia, stroke and traumatic brain injury encouraged me to continue to do research in the treatment of autism and sensory integration. In 2011 I completed a clinical study demonstrating that this meridian based applied touch system was helpful in enhancing learning and social engagement for young children with autism. (Mines, Morris and Persun 2012, *inter alia*, in press; McFadden and Hernandez 2010, pp. 42-48; McFadden, Healy, Dettmann, Kaye, Ito and Hernandez 2011, pp. 21-34)

- ***Cranial Therapy***: I employ a number of basic and simple cranial treatment methodologies to soften connective tissue in the neck and sub-occipital area, at the occiput or base of the skull and on the entire cranium including, whenever possible, the face. I also use cranial-sacral therapies. I aim for cranial decompression, spaciousness and the overall removal of restrictions.

- **Engaged Dialogue:** I mirror back to Sophie what I perceive her to be communicating and wait for verification from her. I also invite her into conversations and share my treatment choices and observations with her. I enunciate slowly and clearly and make sure she can see my lips moving as I make the segments of the words. I do my utmost to be fully present for her.

Engaged dialogue is arguably my most important contribution, alongside the use of applied touch. I talk with Sophie intelligently and participate with her in true conversation.

The authenticity of my relationship with Sophie elicits her progressive and increasing capacity for vital and appropriate social engagement. My attunement to her is a learnable skill. I believe that if care providers follow such a path of limbic stimulation that all their other therapies will increase in potency. Sophie's mother says her intimacy with her daughter has deepened because of what she has observed and learned from my interactions with Sophie.

In this book I unpack these TARA Approach interventions and translate them for both clinical and home use. What I want to underscore is that it is the nature of the practitioner-recipient relationship that creates success. A key factor to compound effectiveness is recruiting active and consistent parent involvement whenever possible. Sophie's mother shines as an example of this by treating Sophie at home regularly. This is one of the main reasons why I selected this case study to introduce this book.

Present, relational, deeply curious and responsive interaction and applied touch coupled with active parental participation including follow-through treatment at home are the foundation of the design I present here for the treatment of sensory dysfunction through limbic stimulation. I discuss my experiences with Sophie and Rett Syndrome because Rett's is one of the most intractable of sensory and neurodevelopmental conundrums. If we can point to any success in Sophie's case I believe this represents promise for other sensory conditions.

The general theme of limbic stimulation revolves around faith in human potential and the value of attuned communication in partnership with effective interventions that are consistently applied by aware and present caregivers. This concept is reiterated in a variety of ways throughout this book. Neurological resilience is driven by the power of love that is directly and consistently manifested through attention and skill. Just the intention to inquire into the truth of someone else's authentic experience and bypass your own projections will initiate the neurochemistry of love. This fine tuning that requires so much patience pays off and ripens into real, observable change. Providing this resonant relational field for a child with sensory challenges is like providing miracle doses of a hormonal solution, a completely natural and free elixir that lubricates resiliency. The chapters that follow tell you how to deliver this medicine that has no contraindications and what can happen when you do.

Part One
Awareness

Chapter One
Assessing Sensory Systems: A Primer for the Diagnostic Journey

The three major sensory systems, Tactile, Proprioceptive and Vestibular, define how we feel, learn about and know the world around us. The Tactile System provides the means by which we touch the world and are touched. The Proprioceptive System is the medium through which we experience movement and feel our bodies interacting with the spaces and people around us. The Vestibular System is the way we sense gravity and our relationship to it. It is how we connect to the earth. I would like to explore with you how the dysregulation of these systems is felt from the perspective of the child, the parent and the care-provider who is a therapist, educator or aide. Finally I would like to place the definitions of these systems in the context of the evolving neuroscience that continually provides ever increasing data on how the developing brain responds to sensory input. The three primary sensory systems interface with the external senses that are fundamental to survival: taste, smell, vision and hearing. Touch is also an external sense as well as an aspect of the Tactile System. This entire discussion is necessary education for those who serve children with sensory needs, especially parents. It is also pertinent to a consideration of the epidemiological levels of autism, sensory integration and learning challenges amongst young people. For parents beginning or in the midst of the diagnostic process, knowing about the sensory systems is a principle advantage.

The innovative tools provided in this book help bring balance and integration to the primary sensory systems and the functions of the external senses. One of these is the clinically tested use of applied acu-touch on specific sites of the body. This method, known as Jin Shin TARA, is unlike any other. It is non-invasive and the quality of touch can be varied, differentiating it from massage or other touch systems. Given this, it seems natural to consider the Tactile System first.

The Tactile System and Sensory Integration

The Tactile System refers to a network of receptors that cover the skin surface and send signals through tracts in the spinal cord to the brain to generate appropriate responses to touch. Sensory information is mapped clearly in the brain for different kinds of touch sensations including temperatures, pain levels, identifying what is being touched, light touch, deep touch, and touch that requires a certain action such as moving back from burning heat. Our earliest sensory input occurs in utero when the prenatal baby contacts its environment in the womb. You can say that the skin, the largest organ of the body, is the original learning system.

The Tactile System from the Perspective of the Child with Sensory Integration Needs

For children with sensory disorders the brain mapping for touch does not match typical patterns. Some children are extremely overwhelmed by touch experiences. For instance the messy things that many children luxuriate in can be deeply upsetting, tags on clothing or rough fabrics can create disturbing feelings and even light touch can be irritating. Some children may, on the other hand, not feel pain when they should such as when touching a hot surface. Others are defended against touch and resist, sometimes violently, even the gentlest affection like tender hugs and kisses.

The term "tactile defensiveness" was coined by A. Jean Ayres, the brilliant Occupational Therapist and Educational Psychologist who in 1964 identified how certain types of tactile experiences caused some children to become extremely uncomfortable and over-respond. (Ayres 1964) Being bumped by other children, for instance, could lead to withdrawal and tension. Touch of any kind can become threatening. This limits how a child interacts and plays with others, experiences their body and learning, and can shape every functional moment such as getting dressed in the morning.

We are fortunate today to have the autobiographies of people like Temple Grandin and Dawn Prince-Hughes so that we can hear directly in their own words about their various sensory responses to tactile input. Dawn Prince-Hughes writes of fearing that other children will touch her when she began school and of her need to take shelter from the onslaught of chaotic sensory stimuli that aroused a threat response. (Prince-Hughes 2004) She speaks in the early chapters of her autobiography *Songs of the Gorilla Nation* of the shelter and relief from tactile defensiveness that she felt in the presence and companionship of those she trusted. She describes how controlling behaviors evolved as a way to manage the anxiety she felt living in a world where she could not manage her exposures to unwanted tactile experience. Like autism spokeswoman and iconic inventor of the "squeeze machine" Temple Grandin, Dawn Prince-Hughes found an affinity with animals that offset her tactile hypersensitivity. Her deep contact with horses was a reprieve for her nervous system. This quote describes her experience when she was nine years old.

"One day I stood on a stump and leaned over the top of the leader (of the horses). He let me slide on and I laid the whole length of my body along his back. I just lay there with the warmth and pressure of his massive body supporting me. I let my arms fall down along his withers. Sometimes we would wander for hours. I had to tear myself away and walk as fast as I could to get back home." (Prince-Hughes 2004)

The power of deep, instinctual mammalian contact as a resource for sensory integration reminds us of the unique neurodevelopmental history that each child carries. This history begins before birth. By twenty weeks in utero babies feel touch all over their bodies. If a child is born prematurely their Tactile System is immediately overloaded by massive sensory input for which they are unprepared. Read about Hannah in the next chapter for more insight into the Tactile System and prematurity.

Studies show that prenatal stress reduces normal tactile responsiveness or can lead to tactile defensiveness, cognitive impairment and alterations in dopaminergic regulatory systems in the basal ganglia, or basic brain. Maternal stress hormones cross the placental barrier and the timing of the transmission will impact the dominant development at that cycle. Stress is one of the epigenetic factors that can influence genetic expression. Epigenetic means beyond or over heritable traits. As the case studies in this book demonstrate relieving nervous system burdens that are habituated from this time can substantially shift sensory disorders. (Schneider, Moore, Gajewski, Larson, Roberts, Converse and DeJesus 2008)

Reorganization of the Tactile System will impact the regulation of the other two systems. This is why I place such an emphasis on applied touch in my suggestions to parents and caregivers. How a child feels about what she touches and how she is touched influences how she feels about her body and the environment. Language changes when tactile sensations shift and are therefore understood and processed differently. The three sensory systems cross reference each other and this is a real bonus, Read, for instance, the story in the next chapter of how Sophie's experience of touching sites on her own body shifts her social engagement.

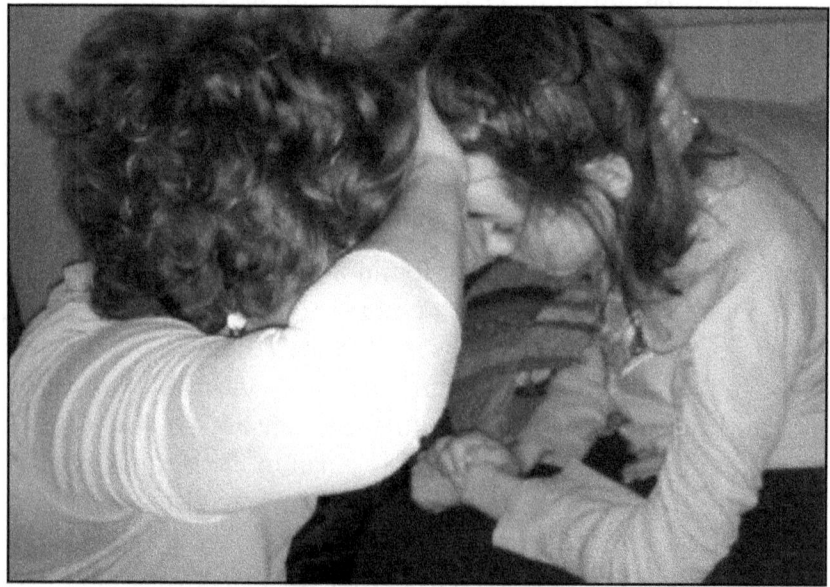

Figure: 1.1 Mother Treating Daughter's Cranium

Look at the photos here that show how Sophie's demeanor and her hand clapping changes in response to the applied touch her mother administers.

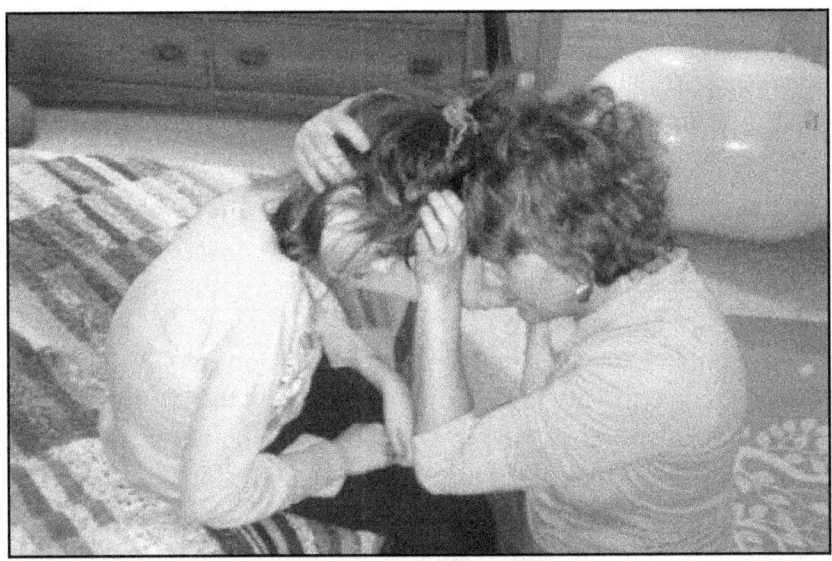

Figure: 1.2 As Mother Continues to Treat Daughter's Cranium: Note Cessation of Hand Clapping

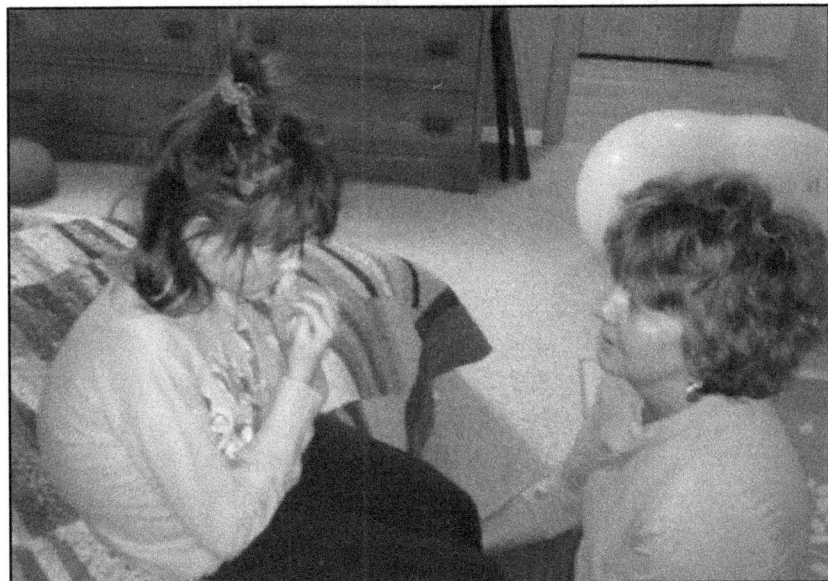

Figure: 1.3 Note Connection as Mother and Daughter Discuss Experience

The Tactile System from the Parent's Point of View

Parents of a child with dysregulation in any of the three major sensory systems are mystified, frustrated and concerned when they first encounter their child's struggles. A parent may feel that their child is being uncooperative or obstinate. For instance, a child with tactile defensiveness may scream or tantrum when getting dressed because of irritation from fabrics or labels. If you reflect on the enormous tactile sensitivity of the premature baby you will have a sense of how a tactile experience for which there is insufficient filter ignites a cascade of discomfort that a child is not prepared to organize.

Parents observing their child's frustration may be alarmed. Alternately, curiosity is the best orientation in these situations for a parent, educator or care-provider. Tracking patterns of behavior points in the direction of understanding. Children, youth, and adults can have extreme sensitivity not only to fabrics and tags, but also to sunlight, water, sand, wind or light. Parents can take the role of principal investigator/detective and follow the clues to solve their child's Tactile System mystery. Indeed the entire diagnostic journey ultimately leads to heightened curiosity and the development of an inquiring mind. Robbie's parents, who you meet in the next chapter, used their curiosity to get to the core of their son's fear of touching what might infect him and thereby solved the conundrum of what was diagnosed as Obsessive Compulsive Disorder (OCD).

All children benefit from being asked permission in regard to touch. In clinical, therapeutic and medical settings a ground rule is to ask a child for permission to touch and explain the intention of the touch. An example would be, "Can you please turn to the left side? I want to see your spine and I am going to touch your spinal column. Is that all-right with you? Is the quality of my touch OK with you?" Parents can, and often must, advocate for this quality of permission asking. The child usually does not have the capacity to do this and some care-providers may not be trained in this way. More physicians today than previously encourage patient question asking but some are educated in a less engaging model.

The Tactile System is often the first one that shows itself as disordered because it is so immediate and primary in life. Vestibular and proprioceptive needs may show themselves later with added mobility. Tactile responses are the primary format for the child's first relationships. If a parent notices that a child over responds to tactile experience the best thing to do initially is to look for the patterns in that response. When parents feel knowledgeable and familiar with their child because they have been watching with non-judgmental interest it becomes natural to advocate for them with care-providers.

Creative aids like sunglasses, softened lighting, colorful hats, scarves and protective clothing lessen tactile overwhelm from the environment. Playful modifications such as tents and awnings are shields and shelters from overwhelming tactile input. When you ask for permission to touch in a non-patronizing way and vary the quality of touch you use in response to the feedback you receive, you empower a child to advocate for herself. Chapter Seven points you to enhancing resources for Tactile System integration. The following section about the Tactile System from the care-provider's perspective adds more.

Tactile System from the Care-Provider's Point of View

My mentor Donita Petersen, PT, always approached her special needs patients with genuine joy and respect. Her primary modality was observation or non-judgmental witnessing. She never jumped to conclusions. She established trust before touching. She looked at the whole child and not just at their chart. Her skill with touch arose from her relationship with the child. Most importantly, she followed the child's lead and had a way of assessing the child to see what to treat first rather than following an arbitrary protocol or a set of rules. This is the sign of gifted mastery in a care-provider. The Tactile System is the one most directly affiliated with attachment so the care-provider's touch must honor that. Donita is always my model in this regard.

Early intervention therapist Neil Samuels told me in our personal correspondence of the overarching value he finds in "learning how to slow down, feel and engage the child where the child is, at that particular moment, with the implicit understanding that what the child is doing is always purposeful and meaningful." (Samuels 2013). This is an attitude, even a way of life that communicates safety whenever applied touch or any modality is employed.

Therapists and care-providers, including aides or anyone who is serving the child, will support limbic stimulation and affect regulation when they are attuned to the child's most subtle movements and responses and not always redirecting them. Because Tactile System sensitivities often show up in younger children caregivers need to be particularly tuned in to non-verbal communication and available to join into the child's experience to comprehend the source of their sensations. Joining with the child contributes to lessening frustration because the adult is co-referencing the child's world and not just watching it.

Caregivers who use touch and feel shifts in fascia or movement, particularly at the most subtle levels, can make comments that are engaged at the child's level to indicate shifts. For instance they may say "There," or "Yes, that's it," as they feel the child shift away from a state of tactile over-arousal into a calm, integrating response. As Neil Samuels articulates it, this engagement "needs to be finely tuned to the child's sensory responsiveness in the moment and must cover an entire set of prelinguistic meanings." (Samuels 2013.)

Neurodevelopmentally trained Occupational and Physical Therapists open alternative sensory pathways and titrate new tactile opportunities for children. These therapists will create environments and experiences that provide children with a broad range of tactile opportunities. Parents will participate as co-learners, soaking up the wisdom, attunement and creativity of these therapists and learn how to capture their curiosity, mirroring and therapeutic responsiveness. Parents can look for these opportunities and even require them. Practitioners who serve their children should meet this standard and parents need never settle for anything less, no matter what their financial resources.

In addition to interacting with children where and as they are to enhance Tactile System balance, care providers should also be able to communicate to parents how to understand their child's Tactile System. They will differentiate between sensory seekers and sensory avoiders and provide appropriately designed therapeutic options for both. The multisensory opportunities in their environment can be transferred easily to home life. There are so many ways to stimulate and subdue sensory filters and most of the tools and supports are already available at home. They do not need to be expensive. You can blow bubbles, drink through multicolored and multi-shaped straws, feel different textures that are on carpets, chairs, fabrics, balls or stuffed animals. You can roll on differently shaped surfaces like mats made of various materials or carpets, exercise balls or outdoors on grasses of different lengths and shapes. Parents will inevitably enjoy the expansion and exploration of the tactile world that their child opens to them. Whenever Donita Petersen, PT and I worked side-by-side with autistic children who were avoidant or reluctant to allow touch, I was able to use storytelling and story-making to open their receptivity. See Chapter Six for guidance on how you can learn to use storytelling and story-making. It is invariably successful.

Proprioception and Sensory Integration

Proprioception gives us an internal sense of the where, what, when and how fast or slow our body is positioned and moving in our spatial environment. This is basic to all movement and all movement planning. Proprioception is the self (proprio) awareness of movement. There are proprioceptors in our muscles, joints, ligaments, tendons and connective tissue. These receptors send signals to inform the Central Nervous System about movement so that the body can respond, react and behave appropriately. Proprioception in combination with the Vestibular System that we discuss next keeps us in a harmonious relationship to gravity so that we move with its support. When proprioception is dysfunctional movement can be awkward, clumsy, precarious and frightening.

Proprioception from the Perspective of the Child with Sensory Integration Needs

Imagine a young soldier from a moderate climate who is deployed to a desert environment and is required to wear heavy clothing and carry weighty equipment. At first this soldier is uncomfortable with his huge backpack and thickly soled boots. Then, after months of practice, he finally becomes somewhat more accustomed to moving on sandy terrain in hot weather wearing the kind of clothing one would need for a snowstorm. When he returns home to his moderate climate this soldier no longer has this equipment nor does he have his defensive, protective responsibilities. He moves awkwardly, no longer familiar with the size and shape of his body. He is wary. Everything is new, just as it was when he deployed, and his body feels strange again even though he is on familiar terrain. This soldier, both at deployment and upon return, experiences what many children with a disabled Proprioceptive System experience. They are like travelers with big suitcases walking down narrow aisles trying to find a place where it is comfortable but fearful that they will either be injured or will inevitably injure someone else. Neither their bodies nor their environments can be trusted. They live like strangers in a strange land.

Karen Smith, writing about her son Evan in *The Sensory Sensitive Child* describes how he would wander aimlessly, frequently falling down, amidst the options for learning available to him in his Montessori classroom. After years of trying to redirect him Karen discovers the clues she was missing in the proprioceptive background of her son's struggle. Even as a highly qualified pediatric psychologist and devoted parent she had not heard about sensory integration and proprioception. Once she realizes that her son's issues were never behavioral or disciplinary as she had assumed, everything changes. She sees that Evan is struggling physiologically to move and orient. Her son was doing the best he could but his nervous system needed help that was not available until she sought sensory resources like Occupational Therapy. (Smith 2004 & 2010, p. 38)

Proprioception from the Parent's Point of View

As Karen's story reveals one of the greatest blessings of educating adults, especially parents, about sensory processing is that it helps them get inside a child's reality. Labels like "lazy," "awkward," "whiney," "shy," "pushy," "anxious," "defiant," and "oppositional" become veils that once moved aside reveal the unique textures and dimensions of a young person's somatic responses to their bodies and the world around them. Portals of curiosity and empathy open, making it possible for adults to become empowered stewards for children. Then adults can support children to be successful and maximize their potential.

When adults learn about what children are experiencing on a sensory level and begin to put accommodations in place for them rather than prohibitions, things shift. Young children, especially those without language development, cannot communicate the magnitude of their struggles to function in their environments except through their sounds and behavior. Psychologists and even physicians without training in sensory integration are often unaware of the sensory dimension. Many parents discover sensory resources only after walking a long path of agonizing confusion and daily exhaustion and discouragement. The purpose of this book is to shorten the distance and bring accessible interventions into the lives of children with sensory needs sooner. Especially when the external senses like sight and hearing appear to function normally, parents through no fault of their own, cannot easily perceive the proprioceptive or vestibular needs of their children. Education is required to notice how a child is revealing their proprioceptive inefficiency.

Autism Spectrum and other Pervasive Developmental Disorders frequently bring with them sensorimotor difficulties, particularly in the area of proprioception and praxis or movement planning. When parents are informed of this aspect of their child's needs they can direct their attention to finding specific sensory therapies that will, in the long run, support the whole child. It is through proprioception that we decide how to move and whether to contract or stretch muscles and joints for action and postural alignment. Proprioception helps us account for the body parts engaged in activity so we can calculate how to physically perform an action.

The intricate brain-body network of the Proprioceptive System navigates our movements. It makes constant adjustments, collaborating with vision and balance for the millions of complex functional shifts required for play, activities and learning. Because proprioception operates innately, attending to it requires heightened awareness. This is a learning curve for most parents who are not trained in Occupational or Physical Therapies. Waking up to this dimension of behavior is enlightening. Adults gain new respect for children who have been struggling with proprioceptive difficulties. They also advance their own knowledge of the miracles of human life and stop taking functions they perform easily for granted. I encourage parents to not hesitate to be inquisitive and to research freely to maximize their sensitivity to and perceptions of proprioception. Tuning in to the Proprioceptive System and feeling competent to discuss it will enhance advocacy and the creativity needed to build niche constructions. (See Chapter Seven for more information on niche construction.) This awareness will also make it possible for parents to organize their child's space and daily life effectively.

Proprioception from the Caregiver's Perspective

The movement planning aspect of proprioception is called praxis. Caregivers who can creatively arouse movement planning for someone like Sophie, for instance, will uplift the quality of her life. If that therapist can, in addition, communicate to parents how mobility can be increased and optimized with safety, benefit and satisfaction, the child's capacity to learn and engage with others will simultaneously be enhanced. Because of the genetic mutation in Rett's disorder, stimulating praxis is particularly challenging but Sophie has shown that it is possible. Through therapeutic riding that is facilitated by an Occupational Therapist, movement therapies, yoga, swimming and exercise Sophie has evolved into an active adolescent who can orient towards movement and request it.

With support and assistance Sophie moves in her world. She is active at home, in school, in nature and in her community. This is promising for other girls with Rett's and, by extension, also for the broad spectrum of young people with severe autism and sensory struggles. An essential discovery that I, along with Sophie's mother and other parents of children with motor planning difficulties, have made is that movement and movement planning helps to cultivate attention, alertness and engagement. Because children with proprioceptive difficulties are seen as awkward or clumsy they may refrain from movement or be hesitant about it and their parents may feel this is a safer way to go. However the opposite is actually true. If playful, movement is incorporated before and after therapies of any kind therapeutic benefits are optimized. The movement might be dancing or bouncing, climbing stairs or stretching after Speech Therapy or cranial treatment. This time is well spent because movement is an integrating force. It is true that this movement often has to be invited and supervised but it is not true that it has to be avoided.

Caregivers have the daunting task of keeping up with the research that advances apace alongside revelatory insights into the workings of the brain. A good caregiver will investigate enthusiastically to unearth creative options for proprioception while making sure they meet clinical standards and are safe. Interventions that enhance movement planning simultaneously advance learning and socialization and the informed caregiver will be attentive to this.

Proprioception is synonymous with the key experiences of childhood that include exploring the environment at home and in nature and playing with other children. Well-designed therapy will vitalize these experiences for children with sensory needs so that they do not feel excluded. Neurodevelopmentally trained Physical Therapists can help with praxis by identifying structural as well as mechanical restrictions and implementing sequential treatment, carefully following the child's tolerance, to maximize function.

Praxis is often derailed for children by an influx of conflicting streams of sensory feedback. The story of Daniel Dearborn in Chapter Six is an example of this. Therapeutic avenues that heighten the capacity to attend to movement goals and include satisfying intrinsic feedback are blessings for the sensory needs child. Mirroring and validating the child's capacity cultivates motivation and a strong sense of self. The caregivers who enhance the child's success by identifying it, perhaps simply by saying, "Yes, like that," deepen the child's internal awareness of sensory integration. It is not necessary to be effusive. In fact, excessive or dramatic comments may be distracting. The attuned therapist will mirror in the precise way that the individual child can absorb. For some children, for instance, a strong validation is right.

The Vestibular System and Sensory Integration

The primary sensory systems are designed for optimum functioning and success in overcoming threats and obstacles. This suggests that a child with inefficiencies in any of the primary systems has a significantly greater vulnerability in life. This is especially true when there are disturbances in the Vestibular System. The story of Emma in Chapter Eight illustrates this.

The receptors for the Vestibular System are in the hair cells of the inner ear which is literally the vestibule, or the entryway, for all movement registration, whether fine or gross. The Vestibular System provides us with an instant by instant report on our relationship to gravity. Whenever head position, eye focus, attention or body rotation shifts, the Vestibular System sends signals to reorient, primarily to the neural structures that control eye movements and to the muscles that keep us upright. This ever changing diary evolves constantly. All changes in the environment, such as moving from indoors to outdoors, for instance, demand vestibular reorganization. Just as the Tactile System is fundamental to our first relationships through the touch we experience with mother or the primary caregiver, so is the Vestibular System fundamental to our relationship to the earth itself. Our bodies look for this relationship to gravity just as we root for the mother's breast after birth.

The Vestibular System from the Perspective of the Child with Sensory Integration Needs

Through the Vestibular System the inner ear becomes the relay station for movement messages that are sent to the nervous system. Movement sensations or vibrations are the signals for this instant messaging. The Vestibular System orients the child in the world as she grows and moves away from the protected embrace of early life. This evolution means that independence requires differentiating our movement from the movement of others or movements in the environment that surround us. If this is not a simple process then there is chaos, confusion and fear. The quest for stability and balance is endless. Mothers' lore abounds with ways to soothe restless, tired children through movement. These remedies do not work for children with vestibular disturbances.

The name of the place in the inner ear where movements register is the vestibulum. Signals from the vestibulum go to the neural structures that balance visual orientation and our relationship to stationary surfaces in the environment or the texture of the ground we stand on. This information allows us to calculate weight and the relationship of weight to the postural adjustments we have to make in order to be upright. The child who is not soothed by rocking and riding in the car may also have low muscle tone, making it difficult for him to feel stable. He may be nauseated and therefore irritated, and he will avoid activities that require going up and down like see-saws and swings. From the child's perspective this is disarming and distressing as he sees other children enjoying these activities together. He feels excluded but he does not know why.

Being in a dark place may also cause this child alarm because he cannot see to balance himself. He may cling to an adult or become startled when physically moved. Or, on the other extreme, he may excessively seek movement because he needs it to stimulate his under-responsiveness.

Most children learn through engaged, active, multi-directional play. A child with vestibular disorders will be disoriented by all of these and will not be able to participate without guidance. His vulnerability leads to shyness and hesitancy. If he is hypo-sensitive then his hyperactivity will be distracting and troubling. These are advertisements that he needs help and it is our job to read them.

The Vestibular System from the Parent's Perspective

Parents may see the child with Vestibular System needs as slow, wimpy, reluctant, accident prone and unresponsive to their encouragement to play. Or the child may be called hyperactive, inattentive or unresponsive to discipline. He may act and not listen so it appears he is disregarding instruction. There may be concerns about his motor learning. This child may be at a loss when on vacation or when he enters a new play environment. His parents may assume that he is fearful when he is actually trying to orient.

The Vestibular System provides a core sense of somatic security so when it is disturbed a child seems emotionally and physically unstable. Here again it is worth repeating the call to curiosity to avoid jumping to conclusions that could confuse psychological issues with physiological needs. Hypothesizing in a sensory direction makes it possible for parents to discover resources to awaken a brain-body connection that needs support.

The Vestibular System from the Caregiver's Perspective

The Vestibular and Proprioceptive Systems work closely together. The therapist has the demanding task of determining what to target therapeutically. This requires careful evaluation of how the child orients in movement, changes direction, and what happens to him when his eyes are closed. This careful tracking is usually best done by an Occupational Therapist who is trained in neurodevelopment and sensory integration.

Identifying Vestibular System disorders may require a team of brilliant therapeutic detectives. This system is like the sensory octopus because it reaches into so many aspects of function and internal experience. The auditory system, for instance, is quite intimate with vestibular function. The vestibular nerve and the auditory nerve join in the auditory canal to become the eighth cranial nerve. When we touch stationary surfaces our hands and fingers immediately send information to the vestibular organs of the inner ear so that we can maintain balance. The soles of the feet behave similarly, signaling vestibular areas of the brain about the surface of the floor or earth. If any of these functions do not work according to plan one can feel deeply threatened and unstable, anxious, frightened or panicked. Read about Emma in Chapter Eight for a Vestibular System scenario.

Caregivers benefit from detailed reports about the child's movement from parents, aides, teachers and others who know the child well and may ask many rounds of questions about behavior, responses and reactions. The answers to these questions will help form a thorough picture of the specific supports and alterations that will allow a child with vestibular needs to find precise compensations and stability.

The Sensory Systems and the External Senses

The internal primary sensory systems, Tactile, Proprioceptive and Vestibular, and the external senses of taste, smell, hearing, touch and vision, are interactive with each other. They are learning and survival mechanisms that human beings need to function and evolve in their environments. Their intricate designs are organized to make life in one's world, life on this earth, and life with others rich and enjoyable. When any aspect of sensory function is disorganized or inefficient it distorts that individual's entire life experience in the direction of discomfort and alienation. But this is not a reflection of their intelligence. A young person caught in the web of sensory disorder looks to the adults around her, either directly or indirectly, to solve the riddle of her discomfort. These adults will be able to respond to sensory needs most effectively if they are knowledgeable about sensory systems, curious about their children and empathic. They will look for sensory clues to solve the mysteries of their child's distinct struggles and identify their child's singular potential. With the aid of skilled, neurodevelopmentally trained care providers, and with patience, parents are in the perfect position to maximize their child's unquestionable potential. By reflecting on the primary sensory systems and the external senses parents become sensitive observers and are able to track their children's sensory responses. This awareness enhances their advocacy abilities and their teamwork with caregivers.

"There is no way to understand the world without first detecting it through the radar net of our senses," says naturalist Diane Ackerman in her book *A Natural History of the Senses*. (Ackerman 2011, p.1). The external senses are primordial and fundamental to physiological survival but they are also emotional and limbic. They collaborate in building memory. The defensiveness we discussed in regard to the Tactile System can be translated to all the external senses. Each child will weave the external senses with the primary sensory systems uniquely.

The limbic brain is sometimes called "the smell brain" because of how forcefully smell is glued to emotional experience, relationship and memory. A child finds her mother and a mother finds her child through smell so that, like touch, smell is linked with attachment. Smell, taste and touch, though they develop prenatally, also signal our arrival in the world. These three senses facilitate development through the movements of rooting and then hand to mouth, finding and crossing the midline of the body and preparing for the activities of play. In the womb babies hear their mother's heartbeat and her voice. These sounds orient the baby geographically, sending vibrations that teach about location and safety. We see the world we will enter from within our uterine home and learn towards whom we will move once we emerge from our watery space into the light. The interaction of the external senses with the primary sensory systems is obvious and necessary from the moment we are conceived.

Observing each child in the context of their neurodevelopmental history will help us understand the evolution of their distinct experience of sensory integration. People like Jean Ayres formulated an understanding of sensory dysfunction not only from education and study but predominantly from her careful, non-judgmental witnessing alongside intuiting and imagining what motivates children. When I was working on a doctoral internship in a treatment center for people with traumatic brain injury I would, when alone at night, imitate the movements of the patients so that I could walk in their shoes. Parents and caregivers can do this for their autistic and sensory disordered children, replicating the child's experience within themselves in order to more thoroughly know it. Placing this kind of exploration alongside the child's early sensory history can open the adult to the landscape of each child's individuated development.

Parents are in the best position to track their child's sensory patterns. I recommend that therapists assess children in their home environments and observe them playing with their siblings or other children. It was a dramatic awakening for me when I saw that one young child's movement was much more enlivened when he played with his sister at home. He moved toward her with greater force, strength and coordination then when he moved and played in my studio with his mother. This was vital information that I would not have garnered unless I had seen him in a family environment.

Winnie Dunn, OT, developer of the Dunn Model of Sensory Processing, a Sensory Profile that evaluates patterns in the major sensory systems, notes that how children behave in their natural environments is a central measure of who they are and what abilities they have. Along with her co-author Julie Ermer, Dr. Dunn notes that: "Parents are uniquely intuitive regarding their child's behavior and are able to highlight behaviors not readily observable in traditional testing arenas." (Ermer and Dunn 1998, page 287)

The Impact of Diagnostics on Children and Families

The diagnostic process plays a central role in the lives of people living with sensory processing challenges and autism. Diagnostic decisions shape therapeutic directions, financial needs and lifestyle choices. The quest for diagnostic accuracy and clarity is time consuming, frustrating and emotional. It is also exhausting. Ironically parents can become overwhelmed and unable to easily filter all the lingo, bureaucracies and paperwork involved in the diagnostic process. Then they face the arduous search for therapies and therapists.

Even earlier, before the diagnostic odyssey begins, parents have been through anxiety, ambivalence and apprehension as they try to understand their child's behavior. Then, once the quest has been launched parents have to sort out various opinions, multiple diagnoses and even conflicting ones. This journey has a complex itinerary.

The family becomes educated and enlightened through this arduous process. They may begin completely unfamiliar with the world of sensory resources and end up by becoming leaders for others. I am deeply impressed with all the families I have met, many of whom you meet in the pages of this book. They emerge with a grounded assurance and faith that they will find their way through the red tape and lingo to the truth about their child. In the process, more and more loving intelligence emerges that strengthens and sometimes even builds from the ground up the cohesion of family unity.

Parents and families deserve and need to be fully informed as they make their wholehearted efforts to understand and serve their sensory needs children. There is terminology, biomedical information, therapeutic and diagnostic acronyms, and research and lifestyle accommodations to assimilate. The skills of advocacy have to be acquired. In cases where there are multiple siblings with sensory needs the learning curve becomes even steeper as each child will have unique criteria.

The cycle of the diagnostic process may look something like this:
1. Observing the uniqueness and difficulties of your child and becoming curious;
2. Positing and researching sensory processing and autism criteria;
3. Minimizing your child's difficulty and seeing it as something that will pass;
4. Becoming anxious and concerned that something is really wrong;
5. Talking to others and reconsidering your observations and your child's behavior;

6. Seeking opinions and observations of family members and friends;
7. Speaking to healthcare providers;
8. Making the decision to request a professional opinion;
9. Seeking second and possibly third opinions and more;
10. Sorting through the information you receive;
11. Resonating with a diagnosis that matches your understanding of your child and his behavior;
12. Sharing the diagnosis with family and friends for confirmation, guidance and support;
13. Evaluating appropriate therapies;
14. Interviewing therapists;
15. Continuing to do research and exploring multiple options that are available for your child;
16. Seeking training and skills for yourself to support your child and build a therapeutic environment at home;
17. Becoming empowered and inspired;
18. Advocating for your child;
19. Understanding your new role as parent;
20. Developing a theory of mind for your child;
21. Finding support; and
22. Being a lighthouse to others with special needs children.

This is a roller coaster for the whole family. Extended family, care providers, and friends can be invaluable allies when they communicate faith in the child's innate health, intelligence and creativity and when they enforce the power of the family to be a container of love.

As rough as the waters are on this voyage parents will return over and over to seeing the purpose of it all from the perspective of the child's development. Underlying all aspects of the diagnostic experience is the role of education for everyone in the family. Our sensory needs children and youth fuel their parent's education as they are impelled to learn how the brain functions and what sensory integration really is. The most uplifting education is in the way parents learn who their offspring really are and the nature of the bond that they share. Despite distress and sometimes crushing obstacles the entire process is one of expansion. Those of us in this worldwide community must never lose sight of this.

A Simple Sensory Glossary for Advocating Parents

Please Note: This is the simplest possible glossary I could devise to make it easier for parents to understand some of the common terminology they may encounter when they receive a sensory integration or autism diagnosis. I want to underscore that none of the label terminology that refers to neurological or developmental struggles imply anything whatsoever about intelligence or capacity. Parents advocate for their sensory needs children by assuming that they are highly intelligent.

Autism and Autism Spectrum Disorders (ASD): Developmental difficulties are expressed in a variety of ways by individuals who are "on the spectrum." Frequently the struggle is in social and communication skills. This is characterized by varying degrees of difficulty in verbal and non-verbal expression. Repetitive behaviors are also associated with ASD. Conditions that are included on the spectrum are Rett Syndrome, Asperger Syndrome and Pervasive Developmental Disorder (called PDD-NOS, an acronym for Pervasive Developmental Disorder Not Otherwise Specified). Aspects of ASD are motor coordination and physical and health issues like sleep problem and gastrointestinal disturbances. There are many kinds of autism. Research into causation and treatment is ongoing. Do not accept assumptions about autism. Pay attention to your child no matter what diagnosis is suggested.

Bioelectrical Human Field: The human body has an electrical field that can be measured. Its electrical charge is emitted by cells, tissues and membranes. Electroencephalograms, fMRI's and similar technologies read the bioelectrical field to identify illness or structural irregularities. Meridians, the pathways named in acupuncture and related therapies, are bioelectrical routes. Applied touch is one of the systems like acupuncture and acupressure that contacts this field to promote nervous system balance and sensory integration. New research investigates the relevancy of the bioelectric field in addressing sensory integration.

Dyslexia or Developmental Reading Disorder (DRD): New terminology will likely evolve for this spectrum of difficulties with understanding symbols. Dyslexia refers specifically to an inability to recognize the symbols used to interpret language but similar disorders may be about the symbols used to understand math or handwriting. The neurological processing of symbols does not occur in a way that allows the individual to process the information those symbols are intended to relay. This struggle is not in any way a reflection of intelligence. This is purely a symbol processing disorder. Healthy compensations are now in place to minimize the limitations and maximize the gifts of dyslexia.

Learning Challenged or Learning Disabilities: These are umbrella terms that can encompass a wide variety of learning difficulties. Sometimes, challenges are labeled hyperactivity or attention deficit (ADHD is the acronym for these). Learning challenges can be in the category of focus and comprehension or they can be with specific skills like reading (dyslexia), writing (dysgraphia), math (dyscalculia) or other skills. There is unquestionably an interface between learning challenges and sensory processing struggles. Sorting through the developmental, physiological and processing aspects of learning challenges can unearth the deep seated needs of the child and lead the way to enhanced academic experiences.

Neurodiversity: Neurodiversity does not describe any particular condition. It embraces neurological uniqueness and the different ways that individuals express intelligence. Some people with learning challenges or sensory difficulties prefer to be called neurodiverse. Many believe there are fewer stigmas when this word is used. Neurodiverse is used in contrast to neurotypical which is the word that describes those who express what is considered to be a more normal development though some would argue that everyone is neurodiverse.

Sensory Integration: This term refers to the innate neurobiological process of integrating and interpreting sensory input. The input comes from within the person's body and from the surrounding world environment. When this innate process is unbalanced the person is said to have Sensory Processing Disorder (SPD).

Sensory Processing Disorder: This describes the neurological traffic jam of mixed or overloaded signals that prevents the brain from filtering and organizing sensory input. Under optimum conditions all the senses work together to promote understanding of who we are and how we are experiencing the world around us. The brain organizes sensory information, assigns meaning to it and sorts out appropriate behaviors accordingly. When this does not go smoothly there can be a painful struggle surrounding behavior. Sensory experience can be overwhelming.

The basic senses referred to in Sensory Integration and Sensory Processing Disorder are:
- Vision (or sight);
- Audition (or hearing);
- Tactile Stimulation (or touch);
- Olfaction (or smell);
- Gustation (or taste);
- Vestibular (or balance and movement); and
- Proprioception (or knowing one's place in space).

All sensory input is bioelectrical. All our interactions flow out of sensory experience.

When certain processing difficulties are identified like Visual Processing Disorder or Auditory Processing Disorder they always relate to the difficulty the individual is having in discerning, identifying, filtering or sorting the related sensory information.

Trauma, Shock and Post-Traumatic Stress Disorder (PTSD): Trauma describes what one has experienced when an overwhelming emotional event persists in its disturbance even after it is over. Shock is a much higher and more shattering order of magnitude of this experience such as what someone who has been in a war zone might endure. Post-Traumatic Stress Disorder (PTSD) is the diagnostic criteria for this psychological condition. When a child with sensory difficulties has also experienced trauma, such as being the child of a veteran who comes home with combat-shock or PTSD or when adoption from an institution is a factor, then trauma informed neurochemistry becomes interactive with neurodiversity. Some people experience the loneliness of being neurodiverse as traumatic. For others a diagnosis of autism or Sensory Processing Disorder is traumatic along with the process of finding resources. People who have lived a long time with sensory challenges not knowing there are resources for them also experience trauma.

Summary: Pointers on the Sensory Systems and External Senses

1. The Tactile, Proprioceptive and Vestibular Systems are interactive with each other and with the external senses of taste, smell, touch, vision and hearing.
2. Sensory regulation and filtering stimuli from the world around us provides secure function, behavior and social engagement. When any of these systems, alone or in combination with each other, cannot function efficiently there is distress and vulnerability.
3. Children cannot articulate their sensory distress except through their behavior. They are always trying to do their best. When they struggle, particularly when their struggles are relentless, disturbing and make play and learning difficult, adults need to read these messages from the child's perspective. Becoming curious about the child's experience and learning about sensory integration is a proactive, positive move in the direction of creative problem solving.
4. Because research in neuroscience and sensory development are in rapid flux and advancing apace, parents and caregivers alike need to educate themselves and advocate for children accordingly. This includes in the medical environment, in schools and in the community.
5. Curiosity, attunement and empathy go a long way towards comprehending the unique sensory needs and compensations of each child.
6. Autism Spectrum and other Pervasive Developmental Disorders frequently include sensorimotor struggles. Support from neurodevelopmentally and sensory integration educated

Occupational and Physical Therapists can enhance the enjoyment of life and success for these children.
7. Sensory systems develop in utero. Information about a child's neurodevelopmental history that includes prenatal life, birth and the immediate post-partum period adds a frequently disregarded but extremely practical dimension to the assessment of their sensory needs.
8. Through their curiosity, education and advocacy, parents enhance the quality of life and sensory stability for their child by creating niche construction at home.
9. Parents can, and indeed they must, require attunement and empathy for their children in all their therapeutic and learning environments.
10. Diagnosis and the process of niche construction are demanding and can also be so stressful as to feel traumatizing. Parents deserve and should receive needed explanations, guidance and support.
11. The world of sensory integration needs has a language and lingo of its own that parents need time to learn.
12. Sensory Processing Disorder (SPD), Autism Spectrum Disorders (ASD) and related diagnoses do not refer to decreased intelligence.

Chapter Two
How to Use Your Brain as an Anchor for a Child with Sensory Needs

"Early relationships play a central role in the building of the brain."
 ❖ Louis Cozolino (Cozolino 2006, p. 43)

Your brain is a vital, living organ. It is thoroughly responsive to everything but particularly to human interaction. In this chapter you will embrace a new understanding of your brain and how it operates in relationship to children and youth. You will learn how to actively befriend your brain and the brains of the children in your world as a way that maximizes therapeutic potential.

Your brain is not lodged in place like a piece of machinery with assigned mechanisms for singular functions. From the moment of your conception it has participated actively in all your experiences which it records in a multitude of ways. Based on your unique, individuated history your brain signals your body's behavior. You can educate yourself to participate fully in lifelong brain development and simultaneously use your brain as a medium for the benefit of children with sensory needs. This chapter shows you how.

Your brain is a social organism. Relationships are its building blocks from the very beginning of life. The brain is a work of art that is always in process. It is a playful dancer, a friend on a play date, a game partner. It is not rigid unless we force it to be so.

Each human interaction creates a neurological response. This means that how we speak, observe, engage, connect and play with our children has meaning. It is not only what we do with children it is how we do it that matters. As adults evolve and understand themselves, and particularly as we stop projecting and acting unconsciously, the children we know, live with and serve reap the benefits of our awareness. If our interactions are differentiated and attuned, then we can be confident that those interactions help children's brains to develop. If interactions are not attuned, respectful, present and aware then they create the opposite effect and downgrade development. We can choose to upgrade through consciousness or downgrade through projection. While we cannot control all the interactions that our children have we can certainly do our best to assure that positive, growth oriented experiences are in the majority. When a child's baseline experience is securely attuned then the impact of a non-attuned interaction is lessened.

My therapeutic experiences with the children who you meet in this book illustrate the power of resonant, attuned interaction to change even deeply entrenched neurological patterns. The following is one of the stunning interludes of miraculous change that I was privileged to witness.

Hands and Heart: Involvement and Participation

The hand-clapping that is characteristic of Rett Syndrome interferes in a number of ways with development and social engagement. Rett hand-clapping is driven by chromosomal irregularities that over-ride and even reverse other developmental events. For these reasons the shifts I and others saw in Sophie stand out as evidence that it is possible to interrupt habituation with focused human exchange, limbic stimulation and applied touch.

In the meridian based applied acu-touch system that I utilize and that you learn in this book, the hands are an expression of the heart because they are part of the Heart Meridian pathway. Using this framework I spoke to Sophie about how her hands can be used to express and communicate her feelings. I suggested many times that she use her hands to treat herself with applied touch and this led to breakthrough treatments, such as the one I describe here.

I placed Sophie's hands on two of the sites that are used for the Heart Meridian. Her mother and I saw that as her hands rested on those sites hand-clapping did not re-engage. For a period of eight minutes Sophie had absolutely no observable impulse to clap. "Your hands are yours," I said and Sophie smiled in response. Sophie's hands consistently softened whenever I placed them on these sites in ongoing treatment sessions. It was startling to see the radical shift in her skin tone when this occurred. She returned eye contact and did not struggle to move her hands for periods that eventually lasted beyond ten minutes. Her breathing was deep and regular and her face was peaceful. Her sympathetic nervous system entered a rest phase and her parasympathetic nervous system stepped up, providing calming regulation.

Sophie's active participation in treatment continues. There is an ever more fluid dialogue between us as she develops into womanhood. For instance, Sophie has recently agreed to cease hand wringing so I can listen to her pulses. I told her that I cannot read her pulses accurately unless she does this and she has willingly complied. Sophie's full participation in treatment and her use of self-care is a hallmark of the comprehensive TARA Approach (Tools for Awakening Resources and Awareness) that I developed and that distinguishes it from other modalities. In the pages of this book you will encounter other children who continue their applied touch treatments on their own and even share them with others.

The Red and the White: Sympathetic and Parasympathetic Nervous System Balance for Children with Sensory Processing Struggles

Hyper- and hypo-arousal, over- and under-reactive states are unavoidable aspects of sensory disturbance. Parents and caregivers get frustrated by attempts to balance the see-saw of these dichotomies. Their challenges are daunting and exhausting and they often feel helpless when distress accelerates into tantrums or melt-downs that seem to insist on running their course. Lethargy and low tone diminish engagement and slump a child into isolation and loneliness. How can adults rally creativity when they have reached their limit? This book is all about how to bring new skills to those moments of helplessness.

While each of the sensory systems has its own healthy sympathetic and parasympathetic expression, extreme sympathetic and parasympathetic nervous system directives are responses to threat. These responses reflect a driving will to survive. Patterns of threat, whether the threat is environmental, personal, or arising from a crisis can become timeless in the brain if it is unresolved. When reactivated these memories of threat arouse the replay of the original hormonal responses. Thus is born sympathetic or parasympathetic dominance, otherwise known as cycles of hyper- or hypo-arousal.

Observing a child's cycles of sympathetic or parasympathetic dominance is the first step in designing effective interventions using the tools in this book. Part Two of this book provides the practical tools you need to invite the nervous system into homeostasis (also known as allostasis). The interventions are not intended to take the place of other therapeutic avenues for sensory needs. Rather they are supplemental and have been shown to enhance other modalities such as Physical and Occupational Therapy. (Mines, Morris and Persun 2012, *inter alia*) Here are some illustrations of how this works.

Hyperactivity and Sympathetic Dominance: A New Beginning

Robbie was diagnosed with Obsessive Compulsive Disorder, Hyperactivity and Asperger's Syndrome. This seven-year-old could spend days without sufficient sleep, perseverating on fears of having infected someone with something, and unable to focus. Robbie could shift at the drop of a hat into behavior that turned his home into a madhouse led by sleepless parents unsure of who their son had become.

Robbie was the poster child for sympathetic dominance run amok, with fear spreading its contagion like the plague. Robbie's face, at the onset of his panic, turned bright red and stayed that way until he was able to calm down which could take days, even weeks. This was the literal red flag that his sympathetic nervous system was in charge. Everything systemically speeded up and he was in a permanent state of alert. Robbie talked fast, his eyes darted and blinked, and his hands were aflutter, always in motion. This is global hyper-arousal.

Robbie's primitive, survival brain mobilized his adrenal system so that it over-fired relentlessly, putting him, and by association all those around him, into a tailspin of action and reaction. What was behind this? His parents were mystified and understandably troubled. They participated in one of my Family Clinics that required completing a questionnaire about Robbie's prenatal life and birth. You can see sample questions from this questionnaire in the next chapter. As discussed earlier, it is illuminating to look at the neurodevelopmental history of each child's sensory development even going back to birth or earlier. In their book *Scared Sick*, public health researchers Robin Karr-Morse and Meredith Wiley discuss the correlation between prenatal and birth stress and autism, including Asperger's Syndrome. (Karr-Morse and Wiley 2012, p. 201)

Robbie's mother described her son's emergency caesarean delivery as a horrific shock that she was still recovering from. An infection had been identified in the course of labor and there was a mad rush to get Robbie out. Stress levels were high all around. Robbie's mom was devastated because she was separated from her son and heavily anesthetized. It felt like a long time before she could engage with her newborn and then she entered the haze of post-partum depression. Remembering this time was not easy. Both parents became emotional talking about it. They had wanted something very different for their first child.

I supported Robbie's parents by giving them the space they needed to realize that they had not failed their son or themselves. Once they felt at peace with how Robbie came into the world and how they had handled the situation, they saw him as courageous and victorious. They saw themselves as having done the best they could possibly do and realized that they were actually without regrets. You could say that in order to help their son resolve the sensory overload of his birth experience his parents had to sort out their own. While this was not by any definition the singular cause of Robbie's multiple diagnoses it was a layer of the burden on his nervous system that they had the capacity to relieve.

We arranged a game that had to do with Robbie finding his way through an obstacle course that he himself created, though he asked us to help him. He had to make his way out of a wide, colorful tent, crawl through a curving tunnel, and meet his mother on the other side where she was waiting for him with open arms, dad at her side. Robbie loved doing this and wanted to do it over and over again. There was a lot of laughter, excitement, and joy punctuated by shouts of surprise and delight. It was a free-for-all for Robbie. No one interfered. We all simply gave him the space to play to his heart's delight. When he had completed his obstacle course enough times to satisfy himself he rested in his mother's arms and allowed me, after I asked his permission, to first hold the crown of his head and then the calves of his legs so that he could rest even more deeply into welcoming. His breath deepened as the applied touch clearly relieved stress from his nervous system. Robbie's unsequenced sensory experiences from birth became organized and integrated in this process. What he could not receive at that time because he was not held by his mother he received now. You could see this resolution through the softening of his facial structures and the balanced coloration of his skin tone.

Children respond rapidly to therapy that is fun, non-invasive and in which they are fully engaged. In this way they do not have to carry unnecessary nervous system burdens into their adult lives. Because Robbie's parents had calmed their own nervous systems prior to addressing their son's needs, their brains were able to focus on him more clearly. Robbie sensed this immediately. The infection in his mother's body had created a stress response during Robbie's birth causing a sympathetic overdrive that then became patterned in his nervous system. The issue of contagion that was associated with his compulsive behavior may have been tied to this early experience. This behavior disappeared entirely after his obstacle course play.

The non-stressed brains of Robbie's parents anchored him, allowing, him to reorganize his own responses. His fears were relieved when he felt that here and now he was alive and well and his parents were happily with him. Robbie's adrenals took a much deserved break and his sleep patterns stabilized. His parents were extremely happy about this! There is nothing like the simplicity of good rest to promote well-being and sensory balance. Fatigue kindles all sensory disturbances. I continued to see Robbie and his family and we addressed other aspects of his sensory needs, particularly in the area of social engagement. Robbie became deft at calming himself. He revealed to all of us the synergistic behavior of the sensory systems and the fundamental role of the Tactile System in development.

Hypo-arousal and Parasympathetic Dominance: Finding Fearless Strategies

Parasympathetic dominance or under-arousal takes the forms of low tone, passivity and withdrawal, flat affect and reluctance to engage. The children who are parasympathetic dominant tend to whiten readily even more under stress. Twelve year old Hannah, for instance, was on the verge of failure to thrive. Her weak core would not allow her to sit upright at her desk or even hold her pencil to write. There were many considerations for Hannah, including tactile and vestibular needs, food allergies, emotional concerns and digestive issues. Physical Therapy was slowly helping to develop more core strength but her family felt she needed more resources. They were concerned. Hannah's weight was frightfully low.

Extreme responses to food can be an indication of sensory needs. In Hannah's case there was unquestionably a chronic pattern of oral defensiveness that Physical Therapy had not been successful in altering but that did change with the use of applied touch. In our sessions I injected another component by identifying, articulating and mirroring what I observed about Hannah in a manner that she could receive and digest. This synergy turned the tide. Hanna, like the much younger Ellie in Chapter Six who also struggled with eating, was born prematurely and never breastfed. As a preemie Hannah was inundated with sensory stimuli that she was unprepared to integrate, and left alone frequently with that global overwhelm. It was notable that Hannah usually retreated into her room and elected solitude over the high-spirited activities of her siblings and peers. While her parents suspected that Hannah was rejecting certain difficult relationships, both her Physical Therapist and I wondered about the sensory implications.

I used applied touch on Hannah's face, by holding softly in the area of her cheekbones using the full palms of both my hands and sliding them slowly down the sides of her face towards her jaw. I did this several times, inviting her breath to coordinate with the sweeps across her jawline. I then asked her to feel her breath filling her belly to satisfaction and then to focus on the emptying and then natural refilling of her belly with breath. This is how babies breathe. Even watching children breathe this way is soothing. Experiencing it is even more fulfilling. Hannah noticeably enjoyed this. Sometimes she could not prevent her mouth from falling open slightly as she focused on her belly breathing. She always laughed softly when this happened. Chapter Five includes additional treatment for relieving oral defensiveness.

In our conversations I never mentioned eating at all. Instead I asked her about her life and what she loved to do. When she answered I noticed when she appeared energized. Whenever her eyes and face brightened as she spoke I mirrored that brightness back to her. I smiled in response to her smiles and expanded our conversation on the topics she enjoyed. I presented her with my curiosity and interest in what interested her. Hannah had an eye for beauty in jewelry and clothing. She loved to draw and shared her drawings with me. I was impressed by them. They were precise, detailed, realistic and intricate. They had recruited her care and attention. She had invested energy in them. This struck me as a significant contrast to her otherwise lethargic state. The combination of emphasizing where she thrived and using applied touch to decrease her oral defensiveness and strengthen her energetic reserves ultimately brought Hannah out of her parasympathetic slump. After each treatment there was always a little more pink in her skin coloring. Changes in skin tone are simple clues to sensory reorganization.

I created space for Hannah to initiate in our relationship. When the parasympathetic nervous system is dominant this is pivotal. The person who feels stripped of energy may feel initiation is not feasible but if you provide a companionable spaciousness, a demand-free quality of exchange, and a witnessing brain that is not invasive they will find their determination. The fear that they won't find it can be debilitating. Everyone wants to connect but not if they feel that connection will not answer their needs. It was difficult for Hannah's parents to learn how to not be driven by their own distress. It took the development of a significant trust in her on their part, and a surrender of their own agenda, to give Hannah the space to find her will. As a parent I myself would be challenged if faced with a similar situation. Hannah made a choice to live when she was born prematurely and she made that choice again. Early developmental issues frequently resurface at key developmental interludes and Hannah was on a life cycle threshold. This was also an aspect of the mystery. With the softening of her oral structures and with more space and less pressure Hannah did find her own motivation and the will to eat. She gained weight and strength consistently. Ongoing applied touch and engaged, titrated dialogue enlivened her. Physical Therapy continued to innervate her core and her relationship with her PT was similarly nutritive. Her determination to be herself re-emerged in the space provided. As she added weight she demonstrated increasing capacities to engage and participate. She discovered, for herself, a burgeoning relationship to substance and to gravity.

Early experiences of threat condition neuronal consolidation and contribute to sensory disorders. Parents and caregivers can form a triage with therapists to offer a variety of alternatives to habituated behavior. During pubescence or adolescence parents may have to step out of the picture to concede the arena for growth. This can be a leap of faith. The sequenced touch that Hannah's attuned PT used to strengthen her midline and the gentle, progressive softening of her facial structures in combination with the recognition she received spoke to Hannah. With a more organized and supported Tactile System, and the simultaneous bolstering of her developmental initiative, her other primary systems came on board.

The Rhythms of Life: Honoring Selfhood

The simple act of honoring a child's right to choose how and when treatment proceeds, ends and transitions is a step in the direction of relational resonance and limbic stimulation that promotes brain development. Rhythms of interaction, touch exchanges, communication, learning and action are fundamental components of selfhood that shape sensory integration. Caregivers can learn to recognize the unique signals and patterns of each child, whether verbal or non-verbal, to establish verifiable channels of agreement about these rhythms.

Consistently invite collaborations in treatment. Imagine the relief of being included in this way and the sense of being devalued when you are not. Children's personalized developmental rhythms must be acknowledged. The story that follows, about Carlos and his mother, demonstrates the power of building selfhood by integrating advocacy with trusting your child's particular developmental rhythms. The biographies of neurodiverse individuals portray the irreplaceable value of parental endorsement as ballast in confronting erroneous perceptions of sensory disorders.

Advocacy Promotes Sensory Integration

Carlos had lived much of his young life with a mix of learning, sensory and physical afflictions that were just starting to dissipate as he headed into his seventh year. Severe headaches, explosions of rage and tantrums, hyperactivity and sensory seeking had given his life a circus like rhythm. One thing that dependably soothed him was a stuffed animal that he carried everywhere, though he usually hid it in his backpack. At a visit to his pediatrician Carlos felt he needed to bring his stuffed animal out and hold it. The pediatrician asked him why he "still" needed his stuffed animal. Fortunately Carlos' mom rallied to her son's defense. She declared that Carlos was doing beautifully and that if he needed his stuffed animal, he could have it. It was his to take out, she declared whenever he needed it. What a relief for Carlos to have this burden of shame taken off so readily. The experience immediately gave him a sense of protection and safety.

In a Family Clinic just prior to this incident Carlos' mom

had shared her struggle with feeling intimidated by some of the medical professionals she met in her search for healthcare services for her special needs child. For the first time she had the chance to process for herself what her son's diagnoses meant for him and her family. She expressed feelings of inadequacy as she tried to grapple with the language the doctors used and her sense of guilt about Carlos' unbounded behaviors. Carlos' mom doubted her attunement to her son and thought others knew better even when she had a strong internal sense of knowing and an instinctual connection to Carlos. Finding her voice was both her evolution and the password to her son's. Andrew Solomon, in his epic investigation into difference, *Far From the Tree,* notes that "The closeness with which a parent observes can be as powerful as the expertise with which a physician observes." Parents need to value their expertise, as valid science. "Medicine," Solomon continues, "is often unprepared for parental perspectives that do not align with an illness model." (Solomon 2012, p. 257)

The very experience of the self is established through the validation of personal rhythm. Things will always go more easily with a child who has a coherent sense of safety and self. Starting, stopping and changing direction that is inclusive of the child's inner world promotes the strength of the sensory, motor and visceral grid which is the infrastructure for later cognitive development.

There is a long term brain building result that comes from integrating a child's rhythms into their relational experiences and trusting individuated developmental cycles. The family and treatment environments that are attuned and respectful become rhythmic shelters from the accelerated activity of a sensory overload world. By honoring a child's rhythms and having faith in who the child or young person is we help them find a route to self-regulation.

Anchoring A Sensory Needs Child through Right Hemispheric Resonance

This book provides parents and care providers with tools to anchor children through right hemispheric resonance or attuning to the child's emotional and visceral experience. I have created a sensory integration formula using your aware relationship and your healing hands. This recipe for sensory integration awakens the positive neurochemistry that comes from being seen, heard and invited into participation in the world. Anchoring requires that the adults in the child's world observe or witness the child without projection and assumptions.

The origins of sensory integration, as we learned in Chapter One, are in utero, along with neural development. The foundation for reflexive communication through movement and respiration, even the capacity to express responsive feeling, is in place before we are born. For this reason I recommend that all parents and care-givers of special needs children take into consideration the gestational period of a child's life to fully comprehend them and enter their world.

Anchoring in a strong sense of self, attachment to a safe relationship, the felt sense of being seen that is validated by attuned interaction, respecting the child's rhythms of interaction all produce a more organized and self-regulating nervous system. This is what we can offer our children simply through our brain to brain contact with them. There is no question that providing this level of awareness and exchange is time intensive. It cannot be hurried. The benefits compound through our consistent attention, continuity and follow-through. Parents and care-givers are the child's historians, carefully tracking subtle shifts in sensory responses, interpersonal relationships, play and sleep patterns, health, movement and expression. The time invested reaps the rewards of selfhood and sensory integration for the child and intrinsic joy and fulfillment for the adults.

Summary: Pointers on How to Use Your Brain to Anchor a Neurodiverse Child

1. See and experience your adult brain as resilient and responsive.
2. Knowing that relationships shape development, interact accordingly.
3. Explore your own patterns of sympathetic and parasympathetic nervous system dominance as a way to comprehend

these arms of the nervous system. Then do the same for the children in your care.

4. Investigate the role of your prenatal and birth experiences in shaping your development. This may require asking some questions of your parents, relatives and siblings. See the list of questions you might consider that is provided in the next chapter. Then reflect on those circumstances for children. Put this early history into your perspective on sensory integration.

5. Note how and when children and youth in your care activate you in specific ways. Find and use appropriate mechanisms to sort those responses so you do not project them. Take responsibility for your activation, track and resolve it and you will gain a wealth of self-knowledge. This will enhance considerably your capacity to anchor a child with sensory needs through the vehicle of your relationship with them.

6. Pay attention to the timing and rhythms of the neurodiverse children and youth in your care. How can you honor and respect those rhythms in your relationship and therapeutic exchanges? Look and ask for confirmation that you understand rhythmic needs appropriately.

7. Practice consciously using your brain as an anchor to stabilize a child's growth and development. You do this when you are fully present and empathic. Let the stability of your brain and heart act as gravity for a neurodiverse child.

8. Use advocacy as a therapeutic intervention.

9. Value your relationships with the neurodiverse children and youth you serve and trust the validity of your careful, non-judgmental observations of them.

Chapter Three
The Art of Limbic Stimulation for Motivation and Connection

"As a family living with an autistic child it felt like there was a force field holding us back from joining in."
❖ Arthur Fleischmann (Fleischmann 2012, p. 101)

The limbic brain mediates between the lower basic, primitive brain and the higher cortex and neocortex, our most recent evolution. Limbic, from "limbus," means ring or circle, like a border. The limbic structures form a borderland, linking the old and the new, the past, the present and the future via the motivational regulators of the hypothalamus, the hippocampus and the amygdala. Simply put "limbic stimulation" means arousing motivation through imaginative, creative engagement with the developing brain. Limbic stimulation erects sustainable bridges to the cortex and neo-cortex. Adults help construct these bridges with their playful, intuitive engagement and co-participation tailored specifically for the brilliant uniqueness of each child. Inclusion and co-participatory experiences stimulate limbic development. Exclusion hampers it.

The Playground of Development

Human beings have the greatest variety of feelings and the most connection to and through the limbic area of anything alive. I call the limbic brain the Playground of Development. If you watch children on a playground you will see every mood, every expression, every possible imaginative combination of relationship, emotion and interaction, activity and experience in dynamic movement. It is on this broad playing field of possibility that limbic stimulation occurs. The on, off, fast, slow, pause and stop switches for engagement, behavior and activity are tested and experienced there.

Imagine yourself in a beautiful park with intriguing play structures, bountiful trees and wide lawns, different kinds of swings, sand-boxes and inviting sculptures built for children to climb, colorful tunnels and challenging rope ladders. Perhaps it is a lovely spring afternoon, or a brisk autumn day. See yourself there with your child or with children you know, playing actively, participating with the children, encouraging them to explore, take healthy risks, helping them share cooperatively. This is what limbic stimulation looks like.

Frequently our neurodiverse children are sitting on the sidelines at playgrounds, watching or disconnected and alone. Loneliness is the polar opposite of motivation. Exclusion is a negative player on the developmental playground. The isolation-exclusion issue will be explored from the standpoint of individuality, selfhood and society in the next chapter. Here we look at it from the standpoint of brain development for children who struggle to organize their sensory experiences. Inclusion and socialization are leading concerns for the growing number of children with sensory processing difficulties including those on the autism spectrum. When a child's sensory processing is disrupted in any of the principal areas of smell, taste, touch, sight, sound, movement, balance and proprioception then there is an impact on engagement in social activities and interaction with others. Distraction, discomfort, and unique responses to touch, sound and light disturb and isolate a child from others. Attending resourcefully to these interruptions in social flow can move the child closer to inclusion. My research indicates that thresholds can be altered in a positive direction by limbic stimulation that promotes healthy social engagement. This book contains multiple examples of how this happens using the empowering tools I provide.

The Eyes Have It

I introduced this book with a description of Sophie's eyes. Her eyes drew me into her world. They also became one of our primary mediums of communication and relationship. By directing her eye gaze Sophie could tell me what she was interested in, what she wanted or needed and even what she was thinking about. I would articulate my understanding of her eye language and she would respond with her eyes. Blinking, closing her eyes, narrowing or widening her eyes, letting her emotions come through her eyes (love, delight, fear, anger, sadness, hunger, confusion, disgust), Sophie made contact with me and with others who were paying attention.

John Elder Robison aptly titled his gripping revelation about his Aspergian world *Look Me in the Eye*. (Robison 2008, first published 2007) The title, like the program for learning challenges called Project Eye to Eye, is a plea for the limbic stimulation that comes from seeing someone as whole rather than broken. Compassionate seeing fosters healthy development and eliminates the trial of ostracism. The need is even greater for those who are non-verbal.

Sophie's frequency of eye messages increased noticeably once we started responding to them in our interactions. Visual pathways are an access route for limbic stimulation and you can't walk down that route alone. It requires at least two people: a sender and a receiver. It is a partnership. Our eyes are our first sensory regulators. It is through them that we are welcomed into this world at birth. The quality of that initial, primary eye contact is imprinted deeply at an implicit level. Eye contact sends the biological signal for postnatal neurological development. If eye contact does not occur at this juncture then that sensory experience can be replicated later. This chapter will tell you how to do that repatterning. See especially the story about Sergei later in this chapter in this regard.

Eye contact can be used as an intervention to support sensory integration, neurological repatterning and brain development. It is especially effective in combination with the applied touch applications provided in this book. Not all neurodiverse children will allow or engage in sustained eye contact. Nevertheless adults can invite gentle, brief eye contact and even though it seems we are not always well received, there is a benefit to this offering especially if it is repeated. The benefits of perseverance can present themselves at the most unexpected moments in miracles large and small that have evolved from a background of patience and consistency.

Arthur Fleishman joined with his daughter Carly Fleishman, who is autistic, to record their family's journey with autism in *Carly's Voice*. (Fleischmann 2012) This electrifying book reveals the stunning value in not prejudging neurodiversity. In retrospect Arthur Fleischman saw that his autistic daughter's communication breakthrough came because two key therapists "never stopped thinking about Carly, they kept coming up with new suggestions and creative ideas, even when they were off the clock." (Fleischmann 2012, p.115) It was to these two therapists that Carly first began to "speak" by typing. Through her perseverance and faith Carly's wonderful mind was freed from loneliness. The inaccurate prognosis of "developmental delay," was refuted by Carly herself. Described as "cognitively impaired" by "experts," Carly revealed her exceptional intelligence and maturity in cogent, fully formed and sophisticated language.

In treating Sophie and others who are nonverbal I make it a point to look into their eyes when I speak and to speak clearly so that they can see my lips moving. This way they can learn how words are formed. Many nonverbal children have intact vocal systems and do choose to speak on occasion. Even without speaking out loud, hearing the flow of words and seeing how they are formed enhances the understanding of them and supports communication. I use eye contact to assure conversational inclusion. I do not talk to parents about a child when the child is present and can be spoken to directly. I situate myself so that I am talking to a child at their height without standing above them. I assume their intelligent attention to everything that is happening. I never use baby talk or with forced exuberance. I employ an intelligent vocabulary. I wait and look for replies in the form of expression through the eyes, gestures, movements and sounds. I validate my understanding of responses through language, action and eye contact. Inclusion in the form of attending, looking and validating equals limbic stimulation. It promotes social engagement and a sense of worth. It implies value. These experiences are the antidotes to loneliness and exclusion.

If you pay attention to the singular and unique minds of sensory needs children and enter their internal worlds, their individuality becomes apparent. Being seen with compassionate curiosity and sincere interest will in itself calm the child's nervous system and stimulate limbic functions. The experience of being truly seen also spurs developmental momentum in the nervous system and provides ballast and confidence under difficult circumstances when the child may be exposed to rejection or bullying.

Witness Eyes

Parents and care-givers of children with sensory needs can practice seeing with witness eyes to promote limbic stimulation. This is a way of observing and connecting that is free of judgment or projection. What would happen if we put aside the labels that have been pinned to a child and instead see them only for who they are, without a diagnosis? If we, as adults, can cultivate this fresh, curious, present way of witnessing children and youth they will feel its unconditional quality. They will relax and their sensory integration will be supported and encouraged. Forget, for a moment, what others have told you. Look for health rather than disability. This opens a window into limbic stimulation. The change starts with us.

Sophie's gait can be awkward at times. Occasionally she leans on others unexpectedly. Sometimes she makes loud sounds that resemble barks. She drools. She sings and rocks when she is happy. Some people look at her with a troubled, startled or frightened expression. Sense what it might feel like to be seen like this over time. We can also imagine the impact on Sophie and other children like her if they are received with acceptance. This book is aimed at providing education to create a paradigm shift in this direction. I believe it can happen.

One day I discussed all this with Sophie. Looking in her eyes I said, "Sophie, people may look at you and think that there is something wrong with you. I am sorry that they look at you this way. Don't take it in. It is not about you. You are who you are and you are doing so well. There is nothing wrong with you. In fact, you are an inspiration." Sophie gave me one of her luminous smiles and looked at her mom who was nearby. Her mother Cathy nodded, affirming my words. We were all quiet. Sophie's hand clapping stopped entirely and did not resume for ten minutes. We were all absorbed in Sophie's health.

How to Become a Limbic Artist

In order to evoke limbic stimulation in children adults must first inhabit their own limbic brains. This is where your inventive creativity resides, your spark of original brilliance. Limbic functions are communicative, playful, responsive, spontaneous, relational and intuitive. When you are free to feel for yourself and see what is there rather than what you have been told is there then you are in the world of limbic creativity. From this place of freedom you can stimulate the limbic structures of the sensory needs children you know and love. You become like the child in the Hans Christian Andersen story of the "Emperor's New Clothes" who innocently and delightfully articulates the truth.

To stimulate the limbic structures of children and support connectivity to the cortical brain where problem solving occurs, you have to participate on the ground, in the field, actively engaged in the limbic activities of play, pretend, exploration, imagination, animation, spontaneous emotion, sounding and movement. This is the world of "what if" and "let's play that...." Limbic stimulation calls for a shared synergy within the kinesthetic, spontaneous world of all children. This is where neural networks are built. Fluid, cooperative engagement evokes limbic stimulation and a motivation to grow, learn, and connect with others. Neurodiverse children are no different in this regard but adults may have to extend their curiosities into new territory to discover what is playful for them.

Through our dynamic relationships with sensory needs children and youth we help them grow neuronal connectors and receptor sites that vitalize the limbic brain. Facial expressions, voice qualities, vocabulary, attention, contact, gaze, gesture and movement are the mediums that energize resiliency. Curiosity driven investigations lead us to find fresh modes of connection are in themselves pure fun. We use our inventive minds to discover who the children in our care really are. Limbic stimulation is the way of joy and growth. You will have increased energy, satisfaction, inspiration and creativity by taking this approach.

Original Motivation/Original Brilliance

You can tap into the inspirational wellsprings of children's innate motivational cues by investigating their earliest experiences. Parents, therapists and care providers will enhance their understanding of the child's developmental, genetic and epigenetic landmarks by taking into consideration the events, circumstances and environments that framed a child's primary history.

Here are some of the questions you can pose, formally or informally, to uncover this early history. You can create a questionnaire, like the ones I use for my Family Clinics, or you can gather the answers in conversations with parents. Some questions can be translated for children to answer in playful ways. Their answers are always revealing, delightful and disarming awakenings. The case study that follows in this chapter gives you a hint of the joy you will experience by listening to children report about the memories they carry in their bodies. Parents can pose the questions to explore their own responses first and reflect on what the answers would be from the child's point of view. All too often when parents talk about a child's prenatal life or birth they tell you about the adult experience and not the child's. A reminder to see those formative events from the child's point of view awakens new understanding.

- What was going on in the family during the time the child was conceived or when there was a plan for conception, if there was one?
- What was the texture of the parents' relationship to each other prior to conception and throughout the pregnancy?
- Was the child planned or "a surprise?"
- Was conception IVF (In Vitro Fertilization)? Was that a prolonged or rapid process? What were the associated feelings?

- If your child is adopted, what do you know about the pregnancy and birth?
- What was the response when the child's presence was first discovered? This includes adoption and IVF. When did this discovery happen?
- How did siblings respond?
- How did the pregnancy proceed? Any health concerns?
- Was birth vaginal, C-section, emergency C-section, etc.? Conditions? Prematurity? Was baby held skin to skin and nursed immediately after birth?
- What were the relational dynamics during pregnancy and in the immediate post-natal environment?
- Did mom have post-partum depression?
- Lactation experience?
- Did mom stay home with baby and if so, for how long?
- Were there known toxins in the environment such as pesticides, lead, asbestos or air pollutants?
- What stressors were present in the family during pregnancy and in the immediate post-natal period?
- Were sociopolitical or economic events or cultural conflicts dominant during pregnancy, birth and the post-natal period? If so, what were they and what was the family's response?

The answers to questions like these, especially when framed from the child's point of view, provide a context for the child's development and the stressors and resources that collaborate to shape a child's growth and sensory integration.

Considering early developmental experience also provides insight into a child's motivational profile. Parents can make a list of what they have observed to be the strongest motivations for a child from birth or before. What consistently rewards or stimulates her? Is it food, touch, motion, activity, silence or sound? Is it when you sing or when a certain kind of music is playing? What brings a smile to the surface or makes the face brighten and eyes come alive? Is it order, stability, activity, sounds, images, light, darkness, being held tightly or close or not being held, or is it dancing and movement? Observe with witness eyes and keep a journal of what you notice. If you are a therapist or healthcare provider then do the same for all the children in your practice, particularly those who are the most challenging.

Once you have collected this information, what do you do with it? You use it to build a deepening sense of who the child is and what she has experienced in her life which is differentiated from yours. You use this motivational research to learn how to truly support the child in exploring his interests. You acquire the capacity to more thoroughly mirror a child so that a sense of self is strengthened. This is the greatest protection against the long term damages of loneliness and isolation. Researchers John T. Caccioppo and William Patrick in their important book *Loneliness: Human Nature and the Need for Social Connection* illustrate how the brain and the body react to the pain of loneliness by losing function in crucial areas, including intelligence and immune function. (Caccioppo and Patrick 2008) This book beams a light on how loneliness shapes development.

One way I can illustrate what limbic stimulation and limbic artistry looks like in real life is through sharing the stunning experience I had with Sergei, a seven year old boy adopted from Russia who came to see me with his adoptive mother, Antoinette.

Before telling you about Sergei it is important to note that Sensory Integration Disorder is seen with some frequency in adopted children, and even more so with children adopted from institutions. (Henry, Zdenek and Zdenek 2003, pp. 224-229). In these situations it becomes obvious that early experiences of loss and poor attachment contribute to the dysregulation of a child's nervous system, diminishing the capacity to filter efficiently and functionally use sensory input. This was the case with Sergei who was diagnosed with hyperactivity, learning disorders, delayed development and defiance at the time that I met him. Read further to see how these diagnoses were ultimately withdrawn.

Sergei's eyes and body darted quickly about my spacious, open studio. When families come to see me in Colorado they all remark on the calming influence and comforting presence of the mountains and trees that surround us on all sides. Sergei, however, did not at first seem to benefit from this environment. He was agitated and almost unstoppable as he flitted, hummingbird like, about the room, randomly touching objects without paying attention to them.

Sergei's mom was struggling. Her son's behavior was confounding and erratic. Wild tantrums were followed by sobbing melt-downs. He got into trouble everywhere he went and was impossible to contain. He screamed in restaurants, grabbed things from other people, and could not wind down to rest at night. His mom was at a loss. She had tried various limits, consequences, time-outs, loss of privileges, and rewarding his rare non-defiant moments. Nothing worked. Antoinette loved Sergei deeply and believed that his behavior was a response to the earlier conditions he had endured. She was desperate for a way into the world of her son and had faith that she would find it. Her own background had not prepared her for these challenges so she was looking for guidance. It came, as it often does for parents, from her child.

I set up my big colorful tent with a winding tunnel at its exit door on one side of my otherwise uncluttered treatment room. I am always curious how children like Sergei, with out of bounds behavior, will respond to it. It is a symbol of containment, and evokes different things from different children. They all enjoy it, through, and frequently request it when they come to see me. Some parents decide to have a tent in the home after seeing its positive uses. I have seen hyperactive youngsters, like Robbie, for instance, use this structure to good advantage. This would be a very different kind of event I soon discovered. After roaming the room multiple times, Sergei zeroed in on the tent. He circled it, looked inside, and then looked at his mother and then at me without saying anything, eyes blinking, hands flapping, body almost humming and buzzing with activity.

"Do you want to go in the tent?" I asked him. He nodded his head affirmatively and darted right in, like lightning, faster than we could blink an eye.

I expected Sergei to rock the walls of the tent, pull it down or rush out, but he did the opposite. The room suddenly became almost deafeningly silent. The tent was absolutely still. It was almost as if Sergei had disappeared. This was a little eerie. After a few moments I asked, "Are you OK in there Sergei?"

A soft voice answered, "Uh huh."

"Do you want to come out now?" I ventured.

Again the voice was soft in response, "No."

Sergei's mother and I looked at each other with incredulity. What had happened? We were stunned. We waited. Bird songs lilted in through open windows. It was summer time. A warm breeze fluffed the air. In the distance a dog barked. Tree branches nuzzled the building and scratched the window surfaces. The whole structure seemed to yawn.

Once again I queried, "Still OK Sergei?"

"Uh huh."

"Do you want to come out now?"

"No. Not yet."

"Anything you need?"

"No."

"Are you waiting for anything?"

"Yeah."

"What is it?"

"My angel," was the quiet, simple answer.

Again Sergei's mother and I exchanged our raised eyebrow looks of amazement, mouths agape.

"What angel?" I asked, now drenched in curiosity.

"The one who is watching over me. I am waiting for my angel to come. I can't come out until then."

"How will you know your angel is there?" I asked, sitting on the edge of my seat.

"I will hear the wings beating around me," this precious child replied.

At this point I signaled Sergei's mother to move around the tent and raise her arms up and down as if they were wings. She understood and rose from the floor where we were sitting to oblige. As she circled the tent I could see the tears streaming down her face. She was Sergei's angel. It was her spirit circling him

53

even before they knew each other that gave this boy the courage to come to this world where he would suffer alone for so long before his adopted mother came to find him. Sergei knew this deeply inside himself but he could not remember until he was in an environment that resembled the womb where he had waited for his adopted mother's spirit.

Sergei's mom circled and circled and I asked Sergei if he could hear the angel wings beating around him. He replied that he could. Then I asked Sergei's mom to sit at the exit to the tent.

"Can you come out now, Sergei?" I asked.

"Yes," he said, his voice still very soft.

He came out and there was his mom waiting for him with open arms. He rushed into her embrace and nestled his head on her chest. He kept it there for a long time. Then he looked up at his mom and said, "I can hear your heart."

She bent to listen to his and said, "I can hear yours too." They took turns listening to each other's hearts and looking into each other's eyes as if recognizing one another for the first time.

I cannot tell you exactly how I knew what to ask Sergei. I was engaging intuitively in his play and daring to share my imaginative collaboration with him. My link with him came from observing his activity after reading his mother's communications to me including her responses to the questionnaire I provided. I intrinsically joined with Sergei, intentionally entering and following the rhythms of his world on his terms and in the most respectful way I could. I can also add that after years of being with children and families I have come to trust and be open to the miracles that are virtually inevitable in the precious forms of children's play.

Sergei himself provided the summary of the outcome of what happened on that day in what he told me when I saw him about a month later. "I'm not wild anymore," he casually reported. "I used to be but not anymore." Sergei could now focus. He stopped getting into trouble for doing and touching things out of turn and destructively. He did not need to any more. The energy that was unsequenced, chaotic and agitating had found its completion. He had come home.

This is the unpredictable world of limbic inventiveness, the landscape of imaginative play. This is the same potential that is within the fluid, inherently metaphoric artistry that envelopes movies, books, theater, plays, musicals and operas; that pulls you into a willing suspension of disbelief. I allowed myself to fully enter the inner workings of Sergei's limbic experience and I engaged with him there as did his mom. More accurately, I did nothing. I just followed Sergei. I did not insist that he make sense on my terms. I sought his sense and there is where we found the key to his sensory integration. This formula is a total win-win. Everyone benefits. Mom learns, child grows and therapist feels graced to witness the joy.

Natural Genius

Interventions that stimulate the limbic brain and invite collaborative inclusion evoke the natural genius in adult and child alike. The power of presence, creativity and human connection is the stuff of the miraculous. The expressive and movement arts, storytelling, floor play, active mirroring, attuned contact and a practice of witnessing and listening are low cost and effective tools for limbic stimulation, available to everyone. This book is abundant with the guidance and inspiration you need to reclaim the power of human contact for brain resiliency, sensory integration and wellbeing.

Chapter Six gives you a tutorial on the limbic arts with a special emphasis on the wonderful world of story-making and storytelling. You will learn to create stories specifically for children with sensory needs. Templates and examples are provided to make storytelling a route to sensory integration in therapy and in family life.

Stories can easily be adapted into technological formats. They can become videos or animations. The number of videos produced by the neurodiverse community testifies to this premise. Storytelling requires human contact so that you engage directly with a child about their experience. All uses of technology must include this adjunct for positive limbic stimulation. If you employ a technological or augmentative device be sure that it is not used to avoid face to face and eye to eye contact. Nothing replaces the power of human exchange for limbic stimulation. Incorporate human connection by dialoguing about experiences with technology and referencing internal feeling in animated, intelligent and expressive exchange.

In my years of serving families I have found that the greatest challenge to limbic stimulation is not the children's resistance or behavior. It is empowering parents to feel confident and daring enough with their creativity and imagination to be spontaneous and engaged. To empower children and youth with sensory processing difficulties we need to be innovative and present, empathic and attuned. This book is devoted to the faith that adults can rise up to meet this compelling need and that they will have fun doing so. Engaged, creative limbic stimulation is inherently joyful and offsets the strenuous demands of the hard work that is required every day to provide for children with sensory needs.

Summary: Pointers for Limbic Stimulation

1. Play actively on the Playground of Development with neurodiverse children in the ways that they invite you. Share their experience at their level. Do not hover above them.
2. Consistently make appropriate eye contact. Do not be discouraged if children do not appear to reciprocate. Attune to their tolerance and continue to make contact in accordance with that tolerance.
3. See the health in all children and youth despite sensory processing differences and engage with that health. Celebrate it. Put aside all diagnoses for intervals of engagement and tracking. Give everyone a break from the labeling.
4. Allow your creativity to flow. Enter the child's world. Inhabit it with them. Enjoy yourself! Relax your insecurities and inhibitions. This is about reciprocal fun. It will become effortless.
5. Inquire into the origins of brilliance and giftedness from a child's earliest beginnings. Become curious about who they are and who they revealed themselves to be from the time they presented themselves. Be the child's historian and an-

thropologist, tracking their development with an open mind and without focusing on disability.
6. Emphasize inclusion in all dialogues and conversation. Do not be hampered by whether or not a child is verbal. Speak intelligently. Do not use baby talk or be overly effusive. Do not be daunted if others comment that the child cannot understand what you are saying. Attend to the child's responses and have faith in them.
7. Enter the innocent simplicity that is the child's foundation of being. It is from this place of innocent clarity that truth emerges, unburdened by assumptions and evaluations. Great discoveries can emerge from this heart centered open mindedness.
8. Identify and focus on what is present in a child, not what is absent.

Stephanie Mines, Ph.D.

Chapter Four
The Road to Damascus: Changing Perceptions of Neurodiversity

"Everyone is a genius. But if you judge a fish on its ability to climb a tree, it will live its whole life believing it is stupid."
❖ Albert Einstein (Kelly 2004, first published 1999, p. 82)

The way we view and interact with children and youth who struggle to find filters for their sensory experiences influences how their brains continue to develop. Every exchange has the potential to upgrade or downgrade that development. Relational events in the home and in medical and learning environments can, as I believe they should, evolve increasingly towards inclusion, empathy and creativity. Best-selling author and psychiatrist Andrew Solomon's latest book, *Far From the Tree,* to which I have referred before, is devoted to an investigation of attitudes towards difference and acceptance in families and cultures. His is perhaps the most comprehensive and penetrating exploration of this topic ever written. Throughout the book Solomon notes the benefits, individually and collectively, of looking in the direction of identity over illness. (Solomon 2012, *inter alia*).

Daniel Tammet, an autistic man who can describe how his mind works makes a wonderful suggestion for parents and educators regarding encouragement in learning and development. He recommends that when a child makes an error in a calculation that we do not tell the child that he is wrong. For instance, if you ask a child the sum of 4 x 5 and they say 18, we should respond "nearly" and then tell them the correct answer is 20. We should never say, "Wrong." If we say "nearly," Tammet says, the child will get a sense of what the sums feel like and then will be capable of finding the right answer. This gives the child an entirely new way to experience numbers. Furthermore this child will not feel shamed or criticized. Rather, she will feel encouraged. Expanding this model broadly for children with learning challenges will help them experience their innate brilliance. Tammet knows about this because he is inundated with the feelings and sensations of numbers. He found that this is an expression of his genius. To make this discovery he had to understand his sensory overload and how to filter it. As a result of his insights, Daniel Tammet has gone on to make an enormous contribution to our general understanding of sensory integration. Driving in my car recently I heard him speaking on the British Broadcasting Channel about the nature of childhood and the imagination and the role of education for the sensory needs child. His experiences have led him to encourage all children with sensory integration challenges to believe in themselves and to nourish their giftedness. (Tammet 2006 & 2009)

Temple Grandin agrees. She, like Tammet, is an autistic person who can describe how her mind functions. Having been mentored in positive ways to cultivate her gifts she is passionate about inspiring others in this direction. Unique minds need unique ways of learning and it is the responsibility of adults to develop these models.

The minds of diverse thinkers may likely solve or contribute to solving some of the most critical problems of our global environmental, political and economic dilemmas. Neurodiverse minds are already creating new technologies and opening avenues for conserving and generating energy. They can and do develop healthcare innovations and make great scientific and educational advances. The children we serve today are the Temple Grandins, Stephen Hawkings, Picassos, Edisons, Einsteins, Teslas and Mark Twains of the future. Nourishing their gifted minds gives humanity a great resource.

Sensory struggles and autism on the rise may not solely be a disease process. It may reflect epigenetic influences, or environmentally induced gene expression arising from non-genetic mechanisms. Our children could be holding up a mirror to us of what we have created. In so doing they invite us to heighten our awareness, intelligence and creativity. The pandemic rise in childhood sensory struggles is forcing adults to look more deeply into human development and to investigate the brain as a new frontier for science, education and healthcare. As psychologist Louis Cozolino says, "If we are to come to an understanding of the neurobiological causes of autism, we will first have to learn how the many systems of the brain grow and interconnect with each other." (Cozolino 2006, p. 284) Our children are encouraging us to become inspired, to pay attention to them, and to accept and welcome their diversity. They also ask us to examine the nature of childhood, parenting and human evolution.

The Global Wave of Sensory Processing Challenges

Autism is the fastest growing developmental disability in the world. Indeed it is the only one that is dramatically on the rise along with a board range of sensory processing differences that continue to baffle educators and parents. Research such as that conducted by Simon Baron-Cohen of the Autism Research Centre, University of Cambridge, shows that the prevalence of autism spectrum disorders is much higher than previously thought. Current statistics (2009) show that prevalence to be about 116 per 10,000 in the UK whereas in 1979 it was 4 per 10,000. (Roelfsema, M.T., Hoekstra, R.A., Allison, C., Wheelwright, S., Brayne, C., Matthews, F.E., and Baron-Cohen, S. 2012) Baron-Cohen and others theorize that there is a correlation between the rise in prevalence in populations where the parents are involved in technology, systemizing and mathematics. His data is consistent with the data collected by the Centers for Disease Control. (Rice 2009, pp. 1-20.)

Those of us tracking this global phenomenon and its implications for humanity are an international community. In this chapter I am particularly interested in how we can unite and convince others to see sensory differences in a positive and inclusive light, apropos of Solomon, Grandin, Tammet and others. What follows are specific ways to do that in families, as healthcare providers, and as the so-called "neurotypicals." Sometimes a change of this magnitude is best approached by looking at and living our daily lives differently. I am reminded of Clay, a seven-year-old boy whose family was concerned about his obsessive patterns of ritualized, non-engaged behavior. His father was in the mobile phone business. His cell phone was never out of sight. He kept it at the ready even during family meetings and when he consulted with me about his son. It hummed and buzzed as if it were a participant in our conversations. I asked for a "no cell phone zone" at these times. It was amazing to see how this simple change revealed the deep bond between father and son that had been obscured. The dad's willingness to make this shift and to fully concentrate on his son immediately lessened anxiety for both of them. With no cell phones allowed at dinner time, family recreational activities and family meetings the message became one of presence and availability. Identity became more important than earlier illness or business and the family saw the beauty that they had in being together, just as they were. In this family the chemistry changed from what was wrong to what was right just by turning off the cell phones and being with one another.

The Conversion: Cultivating Empathy and Attunement

There has been considerable talk about the need to cultivate empathy in children on the autistic spectrum. I would like to amplify this discussion by directing our attention to how we who care for and are responsible for children with sensory challenges can increase our empathy quotient. Let's begin with definitions of empathy and its sister skill of attunement. This will be followed by a series of exercises designed to heighten both.

Definition of Empathy

Empathy is the rich, fulfilling experience of stepping into the world of another person with no expectations of your own. It is the emotionally and spiritually satisfying awakening to another frame of reference that feels almost like an epiphany when it happens.

This willing suspension of personal prejudices and preferences is altruistic and loving. It is the essence of compassion. The reward is the perception of each child's unique developmental needs. The experience of empathy is essential for successful parenting and service to children with sensory challenges. Empathy asks you to not project your expectations, standards or assumptions onto others. Thus you are required to identify your projections, take responsibility for them and relinquish them.

Definition of Attunement

Attunement is the expressive arm of empathy. The attuned relationship is one in which you communicate with another person using the language and expression that will most readily be received by them. You speck and touch not for yourself but to connect on someone else's terms and for their benefit. Both attunement and empathy are necessary for parenting and mentoring children and youth.

Cultivating Empathy and Attunement Exercises

This section provides exercises for parents, family members, therapists, aides and anyone serving children with sensory needs to enhance their empathy and attunement. The exercises are meant to be provocative, fun and insightful. They may lead you to discover that the distinctions between neurodiverse and neurotypical are relative.

Exercise #1: True Tales of Sensory Overload

In this exercise you share your personal experiences of sensory overload. When I did this exercise recently with a group of healthcare providers who live in a rural area they all chimed in about their experiences of going to shopping malls or large, box-like stores with bright, fluorescent lights, stale air, and information overload. Therefore I adapted the exercise specifically for that scenario.

"I got a terrible headache right away and had to leave," one person said.

"It makes me sick to my stomach," another said.

"I couldn't figure out what to buy! I couldn't even pick the shampoo or cereal that I wanted. There were just too many choices. I felt stupid," said a third person.

It was unanimous. No one from this community had an easy time in the shopping mall. Nevertheless ultimately they were all able to resume the challenging task of buying their necessities and could leave with a sigh of relief and eagerness to get back to their homes in the country. For a child with sensory overload, that option is not there. They do not easily overcome the overload or they may not overcome it at all. Sometimes they melt-down completely. Other people look at a child like this as having a behavior problem. The child is simply expressing what many other people in that same store are experiencing except in a more extreme way.

Imagine what would happen to that child if the people around her had empathy? Children with sensory overload need help, not blame, and so do their parents. A story circulated recently over the internet about an autistic girl who had a meltdown in a restaurant because of the way her food was served. "My hamburger is broken," she cried. The waitress had an autistic nephew. She recognized what was behind the girl's behavior. Not only did she apologize, she brought the girl a new "unbroken" (unsliced) hamburger. The restaurant manager praised the waitress. Customers noticed. The girl calmed down. In fact, she kissed the new hamburger. The family enjoyed their meal. The restaurant's business increased as a result. This is a true story of simple, personal, bottom-up change.

Note how and where you experience overload and what you do to cope with it. If you are stretched beyond your limits do you over-eat later? Or do you compensate in some other way, like zoning out in front of a computer or television, or by reading gossip magazines? These are the habituated, even ritualized ways that we find to manage sensory overload. Most of them are culturally accepted and culturally induced.

By recognizing that children are having amplified experiences of what is actually not so uncommon, our perspective shifts. "Empathy involves some form of mirroring of others actions and emotions," comments Simon Baron-Cohen in his book *The Science of Evil: on Empathy and the Origins of Cruelty*. (Baron-Cohen 2011, p. 37) From Baron-Cohen's combined research into both autism and empathy he concludes that the word "evil" may be a synonym for zero empathy. I am not implying that there is no difference between a neurological disorder that impacts function and a milder sense of overwhelm. What I am saying is that these degrees of difference open our eyes and hearts to allow empathic attitudinal shifts.

The last part of this exercise involves answering the question "What do you really need when you experience sensory overload?" Imagine that someone or something could come to your aid while you are in the midst of your sensory overload symptoms. What would help you the most? Each person will have a different answer and all answers are correct. Out of these responses come tools that can apply in service to children with sensory needs. Here are some examples of what people discovered doing this exercise.

> "I realized that I have to prepare myself before going into a shopping area or a particular supermarket. I can't just go in there casually," one person said.

> "My rescue is preparation which means saying to myself that I am about to do something that is likely to overload me so I need to slow down and focus. I am ready for the experience before it happens because I have already calmed my nervous system. Preparation can also mean not doing too many things right before going to the place that is overloading. I might just do one thing that day and spend the rest of the day doing what I enjoy or what makes me feel relaxed."

This last individual is the mother of an autistic son, nine-year-old Sean. Her son is an excellent swimmer who loved being in the water and always emerged from it feeling more organized and positive. The problem however was that the enclosed swimming pool environment with its reverberating sounds and strong odors overwhelmed Sean and his swimming suffered. He really wanted to be on the swim team and his coach and peers wanted him there too but his sensory disorders were interfering. After his mom did this exercise she had an ah-ha. She changed the schedule for her son on the days of the swim team practices and meets. They used to do errands and shopping before swimming because it was convenient but mom wanted to see if doing less on those days made a difference in the degree of sensory stimulation her son experienced at the pool. It did. Because of the empathy his mother cultivated for him Sean became a champion swimmer and won the accolades of his classmates.

This theme continued. "I have to make a plan for what I am going to buy in the store before I go in there. I decide that I am going in to get this, this and this. I make a list with the brands pre-selected. I have my coupons ready. I make a commitment to not get distracted by what was not on the list or by sales or give-away demonstrations. It takes discipline but then I feel like I am in control and not overwhelmed."

> "I need to make sure I don't go into the shopping mall on an empty stomach. Being nourished is a way to avoid overload for me. It is about grounding. I have to eat foods that help me feel stable, like protein, before I go shopping. I definitely don't want to eat sugar or drink soda."

Are these not excellent coping mechanisms for helping autistic and sensory disordered children function and thrive better in overloading and over-stimulating environments?

And there's more.

> "Visualization is my first aid for overwhelm. I can take care of myself by setting up an imaginary protective shield. I can also pay attention to my breathing. I remind myself that if I do get overloaded that this is actually a healthy response because the environment IS overloading. Just because other people may appear to be OK doesn't mean that they are."

Here is what one of my students who did this exercise said:

> "I use applied touch before I go to busy places like parties or social gatherings. It calms me down and relaxes me. I can feel it working so that I don't arrive there like a victim just ready

to be gobbled up by the wolf of overload. If I get overloaded while I am there I just return to holding sites or fingers in a way that is not obvious to others. It works every time."

In addition to the great suggestions for coping with sensory overload that arose from this exercise in empathy see Chapter Five for the applied touch recipes that my student refers to and others that you can use and share and see Chapter Seven for the enhancements available for sensory modulation.

Exercise #2: Telling Secrets

Do you ever withdraw from conversations with people or perhaps avoid a person or a group entirely because they are "just too much" for you to handle? Everyone has this experience occasionally and some have it frequently. We may feel embarrassment or shame when this happens. Maybe someone talks too fast, too slow, too loud or is too emotional for your tolerance? Maybe what they talk about or how they gesture confuses you. Maybe someone "smells funny" to you. Remembering and sharing these incidents helps you resonate with others who are overwhelmed by people and their behavior. It lessens the hiding and secrecy that comes with social awkwardness.

The adjunct to this exercise, like the previous one, is posing the question "What do I need so that I do not have to withdraw, shut down or hide?" Or, alternately, "What do I need so I can withdraw without feeling bad about it?" Tapping into the creativity that arises from asking these questions is liberating. Creativity is always the richest human problem-solving approach. The neurochemistry generated by creativity and curiosity is like a feel good pharmacy that we carry around within ourselves, but the pharmacy has to be open for business.

Here are some examples of what people have reported in this exercise.

> "I have a relative who everyone says is absolutely brilliant but from my standpoint she is absolutely crazy! I cannot follow her line of thought and she always seems to dominate. When she talks it seems to me like she is totally 'out there.' It makes me feel confused. I go into a kind of trance because I can't plug

into her conversation. So I avoid her or shut down and read the newspaper when she is around, or go into the kitchen or the bathroom. I don't attend family gatherings when I know she will be there. It is just so uncomfortable for me."

"A co-worker of mine talks a mile a minute. I can't get a work in edgewise, so I don't say anything. I shut down completely because I feel so overwhelmed by how fast he talks. I can't find the words to speak up when he does this. I feel paralyzed."

"If I have to answer a question that sounds academic, like the kind of questions they ask in school, I go blank. It is automatic. My eyes get big and my heart pounds. I do this on tests too. I just go blank. That's why I don't like to talk to my brother-in-law who is a professor because it always sounds like he is giving me a test. I hate tests because I always fail."

These are reports of struggles with social engagement. They are magnified a hundred times over for people on the autism spectrum. Most adults who have these difficulties keep them secret. The antidotes to these struggles include awareness, gentleness and communication with others who can listen without judgment and provide alternative options to withdrawal. Judgment entrenches the feeling of self-blame and increases avoidance and isolation. Language, visual or auditory processing disorders may be complicating the desire for social engagement. If we slow down enough to look at these challenges in human interaction compassionately and from a sensory perspective, the remedies emerge, usually in abundance.

Many of these individuals reported that what they needed to stay present in situations when they felt paralyzed or threatened was the courage to ask a question or a way to interject their own communication. They felt assaulted by a barrage of language and sound that seemed to evoke the exact opposite in them: complete silence. Often there were looking for some kind of model that included articulation but they could not identify one. Many autistics feel they do not have a voice and some are non-verbal. They may be unable to process certain sounds or styles of language delivery. They might benefit from a model such as what Carlos' mother provided for him when she spoke up to the pediatrician. When a child withdraws or chooses not to engage we can reflect on our own retreats and sort through for them what could be holding them back. Perhaps in so doing we will uncover the missing ingredient and make a welcoming opportunity for them to participate.

The Garden of Empathy

Empathy stimulates oxytocin, the neurohormone of love and connection. Dr. Kerstin Uvnas-Moberg says in her book *The Oxytocin Factor* that oxytocin increases calm, reduces stress, and heightens our capacity to interact with others. Doesn't this sound like a recipe for the treatment of autism and other sensory struggles like hyperactivity? Dr. Uvnas-Moberg makes it clear that oxytocin is promoted not only by touch but also by thoughts, even without physical contact. This means that we can think in such a way about our exceptional children that will stimulate oxytocin. The benefits go to you and your child. (Moburg 2003, first published 2000)

It is worth repeating Baron-Cohen's statement that "empathy involves some form of mirroring of others actions and emotions." (Baron-Cohen 2011, p. 37) The exploration of mirror neurons in relationship to autism is a frontier field that many scientists are now exploring.

Sensory Abundance

Carly Fleischman, the autistic young woman who speaks by typing dispels the myth that autistics do not perceive what is happening around them while engaged in "stim" behaviors like hand flapping. On the contrary Carly reports that even while humming or racing around the room, she is actually absorbing information at an astounding rate. Furthermore Carly tells us that stimming behaviors are conditioned responses like trauma triggers. If the trigger can be identified then the behavior can shift. (Fleischmann 2012, pp. 121-133)

A revolution in perspectives on sensory integration is being led by the neurodiverse and their parents like Arthur Fleishman, Carly's dad. Many autistic and sensory needs children are actually sensory abundant, a term I have coined. Autistic children absorb more information than neurotypicals and much more rapidly. They usually don't report their knowledge readily because they are organizing it uniquely. Is that something you can relate to? Is it so different from the piles of paper on your office floor or dining room table? I am not minimizing the magnitude of sensory needs but opening a window to empathy.

When I was writing this book my office floor was constantly littered with papers, books and files. When my husband would ask me how my writing was progressing I could not respond at all. I would just stare off in the distance and say nothing. My thoughts were so full, so big and so intermingled that I could not articulate anything specific. I did not yet know where I was going with the complex strands of ideas that were afloat in my mind like multi-colored unwoven threads. I explained later when I could reflect on this process that I was so inundated with concepts and ideas that I could not organize them coherently much less articulate them. It took some time for things to fall into place. Is this autism? Is this sensory overload? Is this normal? The answer is YES to all of the above. This is also a frame of reference for empathy.

Like Arthur Fleischman, parents and care-givers have to be brought to a humble place where we let go of assumptions that have, unconsciously, permeated generations of thinking. As Carly's dad notes, "I was wrong. Carly had been listening, learning and thinking. The far off stares were not signs that she was lost. She was pondering and processing." (Fleischmann 2012, p. 191)

I do not mean to imply that all autistic children are exactly like Carly Fleischman. But Carly is also not alone as a model of truth about autism. Neither is Temple Grandin or Daniel Tammet. Carly's definition of autism is "something I have that other people don't like to see." We can change the latter part of that definition for the benefit of all.

Summary: Pointers for Developing Empathy and Changing Perceptions of Sensory Integration

1. Enhanced empathy is not just the purview of saints. It is available to everyone. You can learn to enhance your empathy for children and thereby optimize their development (and your own).
2. The way sensory challenge is perceived directly impacts brain development for those children with sensory needs. When we change our perspective to be more empathic and inclusive we simultaneously encourage others to change in the same way.
3. Heightening empathy means identifying and relinquishing projections. If you do this you will immediately enrich your empathy quotient. This requires mindfulness.
4. We all struggle with sensory overload. The line that separates the neurotypical person from the one who cannot filter sensory information may be quite thin. When you acknowledge your sensory challenges you automatically increase your empathy quotient.
5. Neurodiverse children become more empathic when they witness empathy in others. Adults have to reveal their empathy to them actively and pro-actively.

Part Two
Embodiment

Chapter Five
Applied Touch Treatments

"Parents are in the best position to know when their child has a sensory problem."
❖ Lucy Jane Miller, Ph.D., OTR (Miller 2006, p.20)

This chapter puts into your hands the basic skills that you will need to balance the most common sensory needs. The applications presented here and elsewhere throughout this book produce immediate and long term positive results. Some of these results may be subtle and some of them may bowl you over. Be prepared for miracles, small and large.

First off there are some fundamental principles to learn in using applied touch with your sensory needs child. One is a map of the body with sites that reorganize habituated patterns. Your touch sends messages to each site to either unload excess energy or fill up with needed energy to restore balance. One site is always held in combination with another. You can think of the sites as icons that signal "upload" or "download". I provide the specific recipes that lead to the balancing results. The sites are located on pathways that are called the extraordinary meridians which are bioelectrical systems that form prenatally. Another name for the method could be acu-touch since your hands serve as the stimulus for balance just as needles serve that function in acupuncture. Applied touch is much more subtle then acupuncture and adjusts itself innately to the receptivity of the recipient.

Another difference from acupuncture is that the map of the body is simpler and the sites are easier to locate. There are twenty-six major sites and many more supplemental sites. We will learn about the sites most relevant for the treatment of sensory needs in this chapter. We will also learn how to hold these sites in proscribed combinations to redirect responses so that sensory experience can more easily come into harmony. The map of the body is provided for you in Chapter Five.

What is most important as you begin is to feel positive about finding the sites and using this system. There are no contraindications. The sites are areas with at least a four inch radius. This is another distinguishing feature that differentiates this approach from acupuncture. Sensitivity to the children in your care innately prepares you for this practice. The connective tissue in the recipient's body speaks directly to the connective tissue in the hands of the provider. Trusting the information that rises into your hands and being quiet enough inside it are the keys to listening to the pulse in the sites.

The map of the body that I provide and have adapted for the treatment of children is a grid of bio-electrically charged sites. The etiology of this map dates to a time centuries ago in Japan but it bears resemblance to the acupuncture map used in Traditional Oriental Medicine. The benefit of this map is that it is less complex and therefore easier to assimilate than the acupuncture map and the way you contact the sites is always with touch. This map was designed for both self-care and practitioner use.

When we hold these sites in proscribed combinations organizing and calming results can be anticipated. These results have been effective in the following ways:
- Decreasing defensiveness, including oral defensiveness;
- Increasing body awareness and proprioception;
- Relaxing muscular tension, rigidity and lessening spasticity;
- Supporting muscle tone and building strength, including midline strength, over time;
- Heightening appropriate social engagement such as in eye contact and verbal exchange;
- Increasing visual acuity;
- Decreasing auditory over-sensitivity;
- Increasing focus and memory;
- Increasing spatial awareness;
- Improving communication skills;
- Supporting relaxation and winding down from excitement;

- Promoting good sleep patterns; and
- Decreasing frustration, confusion and melt-downs.

The entire system is completely safe. You cannot do harm with it. The quality of touch can be adjusted for each recipient's preference and the practitioner's presence and attunement to the recipient will always increase the potency of the applications. The use of applied touch on these sites has been clinically tested in multiple trials and shown to have beneficial results. (McFadden, Healy, Dettmann, Kaye, Ito and Hernandez 2011, pp. 21-34; McFadden and Hernandez 2010, pp. 42-48; Mines, Morris and Persun 2012, (in press, *inter alia*)

Some children with sensory needs will want deeper contact and others will prefer light contact. The benefit of this system is that either form of touch is efficacious. In addition, while these sites are specific touch within the four inch radius will always produce benefit.

The Map of the Body from a Child's Point of View: The Names of the Sites Reveal the Benefits of Visiting Them

You can feel confident using this system with no fears of causing problems even if you are a beginner. You are encouraged to use the treatments on yourself first. All the applications are valid for children and youth of all ages. In fact, there are no age restrictions for the use of this system. If you practice the treatments first on yourself you will have a felt sense of its effectiveness. Children tend to be more sensitive and respond more readily than adults. Applying the treatments is always relaxing. That is the minimum benefit. You are awakening the nervous system's innate healing response and pointing it more and more towards homeostasis with each contact.

Treatment does not have to take a long time. In my clinical trials treatments ranged from just a few minutes to fifteen or twenty minutes, depending on the tolerance of the child. On the other hand, repeating treatment increases its power. You are building new neuronal pathways and melting neuronal consolidation otherwise known as habituation. Habits are not built from one experience so they cannot be disbursed by another single experience. Each treatment is the suggestion of a new option. Each treatment introduces the brain to another way of sending messages that signal new behavior. It's like meeting someone new. You may have a positive impression when you are introduced but you decide if you want to stay in contact with that person after you see them again and again. It takes some time to accept the new presence in your life but after multiple exposures, if the

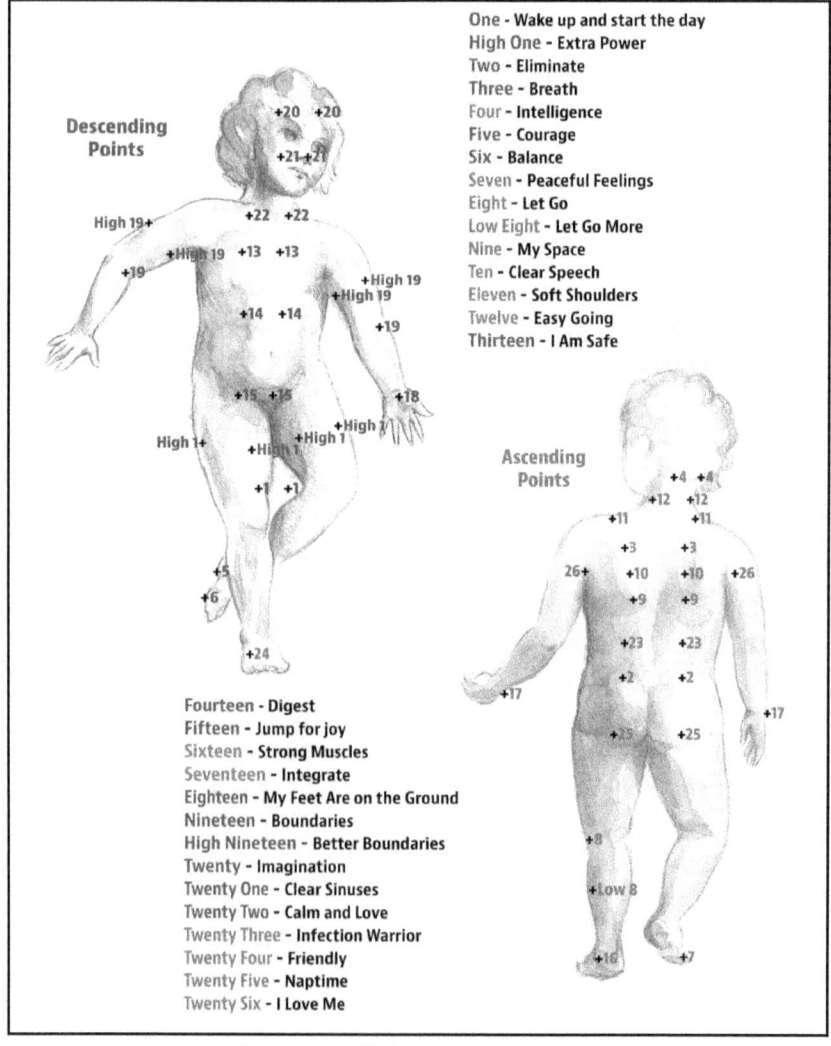

Figure 5.1 Child Map of The Body

relationship feels good, the person joins your extended family of friends and resources. You feel you have a connection that you want to maintain. Life is better. It's the same way with a new somatic experience. It takes a while to realize that you prefer an improved way of being. Then you can let go of the past (who you were before this experience) and enter the present with joy and commitment.

This is not meant to imply that the use of this applied touch system will solve all of your child's sensory problems. Sensory difficulties are complex. These applied touch recipes are intended to support an overall process of self-regulation and developmental advancement that will unfold uniquely for each child. You will see how you can integrate into your life an ongoing simple practice for consistent and steady growth. You will have at your fingertips resources for imbalances that are common to sensory disorders whenever and whenever they occur.

Quality of Touch

The quality of your touch in contacting the sites on your child's body can vary. Pressure can be light to deep, depending on what benefits your child the most. Some children with sensory needs require deep touch. It calms them. In that case, use that quality of touch.

Other children have negative reactions to deep touch. They will benefit more from light touch. Some may want deep touch in certain areas of their body, like their legs or back, but light touch on their face or head. You can vary the quality of touch to suit the comfort of the child in each position. That is one of the beauties of this system. It can be individualized.

As you hold the areas you will "hear" (or feel) a pulse in your hands. This pulse is not the same as blood pulse. Blood pulse has a consistent quality whereas energy pulse varies. It changes as you are in contact with the sites. Inevitably the pulses in the hands or fingers holding the sites equalize. Balance is signified by a round, resonant, and evenly paced pulse in the two areas you are holding.

Parents will find that even after a stressful day with incidents of conflict and confrontation that the use of the simple treatments provided here will take them and their child to a place of calm, connection and peace. If there is no other response than this to the treatments, it is well worth the time and learning invested.

These are the words of one mother who learned this system and even taught it to her sons so that they could treat each other. She had no previous experience with applied touch or any related system yet she was able to be successful immediately.

> *After a difficult divorce, my two boys and I were left in a wake of emotional chaos. One child had uncontrollable anger. The other was anxious all the time. I was drained and desperate. I tried everything. I read books, did research, and used conventional behavioral therapy, motivational strategies, rewards and punishments. Nothing worked. My boys were diagnosed with everything. I even tried medication but it turned my children into zombies and the behaviors continued unabated. We ended up in the Emergency Room at the hospital countless times because of panic attacks, respiratory distress, stomach aches and severe headaches. I was referred to Dr. Mines and the TARA Approach by a medical professional. It saved my family. Within a month of practicing the applied touch on me and on my boys we changed completely. No more complaints of stomach aches and headaches. Our dispositions became calm. The rage and anxiety diminished after two months of self-treatment. This system will be passed on through our family for generations to come.* (L.N. 2012)

❖ LN, Mother of Two Boys in Oklahoma.

Let's Begin! Basic Treatments to Balance Sensory Needs

Proprioception: Sensing Your Body and What is Around It

Many people with sensory needs cannot feel their body and its relationship to the environment or other people. There are simple treatments that can shift this difficulty in perception. Holding the following areas of the body arouses a sense of being present in your physical structure in time and space. Clearing the confusion about this is like taking off blinders or waking up to a new reality.

Embodiment Flow: This treatment can be done in exactly the same way on the right side and the left side. Treating both sides increases the power of the treatment.

Put one hand on the back of the body just above the iliac crest or hip bone (#2). This hand will stay there for the entire treatment.

The other hand moves to the inside of the knee on the same side, just below the joint (#1).

Continue to hold these two areas until the pulse balances in both positions.

Leaving the hand on #2, move the other hand from #1 to the inside of the ankle, just below the bone on the same side (#5). Wait for this to balance with #2.

Leaving the hand on #2, now move the hand that was on #5 to the base of the big toe on the same side (#7). Stay here until this too is in balance with #2.

Now do the same treatment on the other side.

You can do this treatment on your child when he or she is asleep or taking a nap.

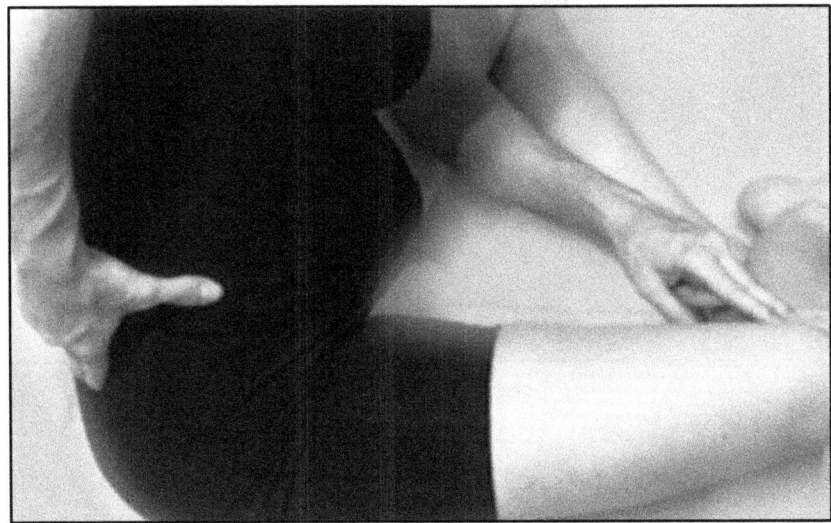

Figure 5.2 Holding #2 and #1

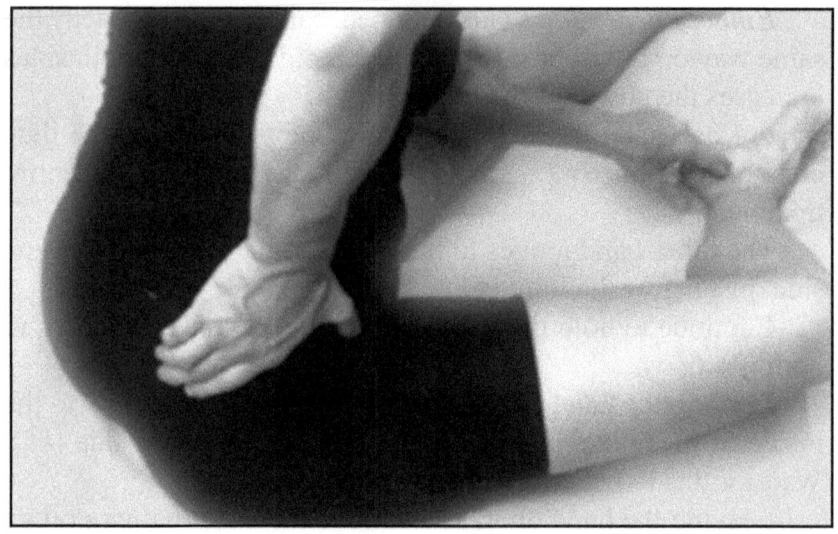

Figure 5.3 Holding #2 and #5

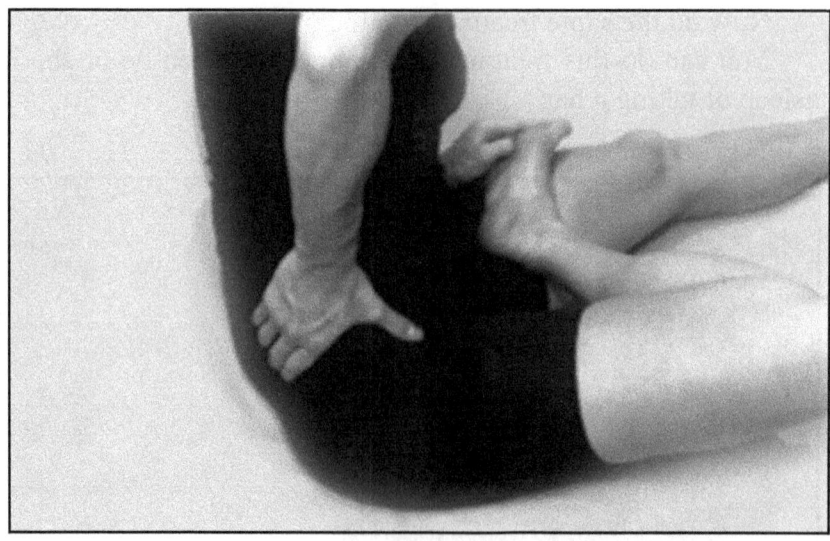

Figure 5.4 Holding #2 and #7

If you find it difficult to do the entire flow you can just hold the first two areas (#2 with #1 on the same side) on either one side or both sides. This will ignite the flow even if you cannot hold the additional areas.

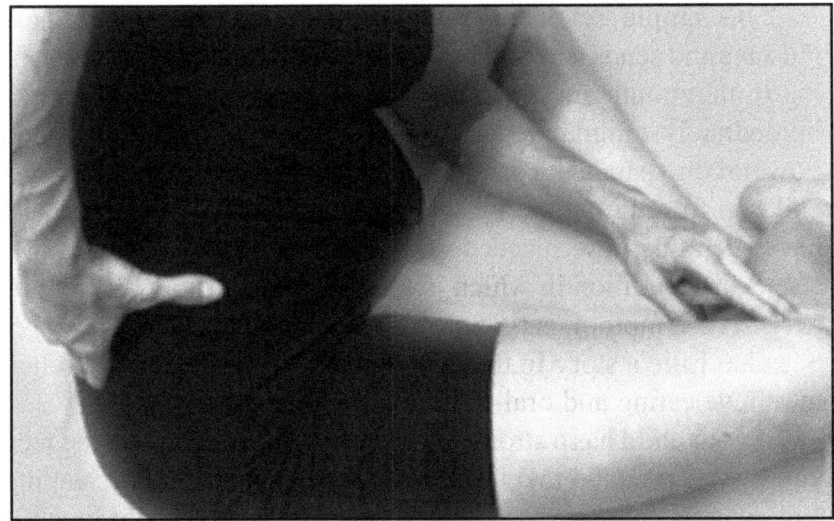
Figure 5.5 Holding #2 and #1

Remember that it is the repetition of the treatment that maximizes effectiveness. Each treatment is having an influence on your child's nervous system for at least eight hours after you treat. The cumulative impact is remarkable even though the application is subtle.

Oral Defensiveness: Relaxing the Facial Muscles, the Jaw, and the Roof of the Mouth

Some children with sensory needs have considerable tension in their mouth, teeth, jaw, and facial structures. This can influence their tolerance for certain foods. It can also dramatically effect respiration, even creating a vulnerability to respiratory disease. Holding in the mouth can mean retaining breath and this is dangerous. Children with patterns of oral tension may also bite others or themselves.

Relaxing the Face Flow: Moms and Grandmas will enjoy using this treatment or flow on themselves to test its effectiveness. When I learned it from my teacher she referred to it as the "face lift" flow because it actually relaxes and softens the face and thereby lessens the tension lines that reveal themselves with aging. One practitioner has turned the knowledge of this flow into a money making spa treatment because it works so well!

This simple treatment speaks directly and readily to the jaw muscles and sends a loving but strong signal to let go. The clenching in the mouth and the narrowing at the roof of the mouth is immediately commanded to release. Consistent repetition of this flow not only stops the damage to tooth structure it also prevents children from biting their own hands and holding their breath. I have seen this flow succeed with children with Rett Syndrome, a sensory condition in which jaw tension and teeth grinding is a pervasive symptom, eating problems of all kinds, and with rage. See also Ellie's story in the next chapter for more applied touch to relieve eating and oral-motor disturbances.

If your child has a strong reaction to being touched on the face you may want to do this flow at night when he or she is sleeping and even those be sure to hold these areas lightly. Light touch is very effective. If a child is awake I always prepare them for touch on their face or head by letting them know where my hands will be placed. Alternately I invite them to place their own hands on the required sites. This is a stellar, distinguishing attribute of the TARA Approach and Jin Shin TARA. The self-care component is sustainable and empowering for all ages and all dispositions.

There are several ways to implement this flow. The key area

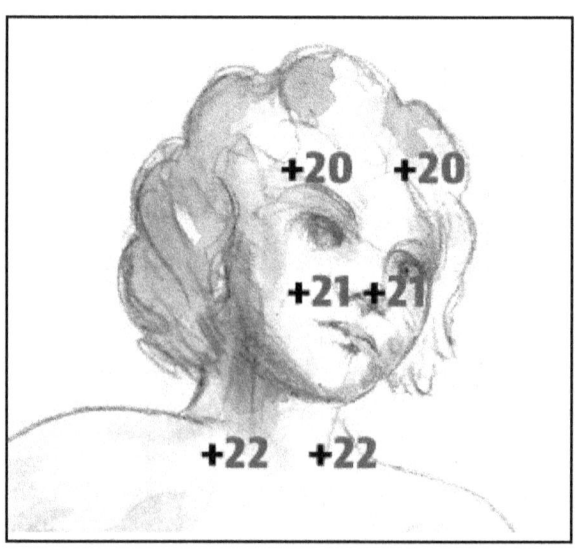

Figure 5.6 Relaxing the Face Flow

is just by the nostrils, on both sides, under the cheekbone (#21). This area can be held in conjunction with two other areas. One is just over the arch of the eyebrow on the forehead (#20). The other is just under the collarbone (#22). You can hold these areas in any combination with #21, on the same or opposite sides, or both.

Over and Under Responsiveness: Evoking Nervous System Symmetry

Sensory needs fall broadly into two categories: under or over responsiveness. Under responsiveness relies heavily on the parasympathetic nervous system. Over responsiveness is driven by the sympathetic nervous system. If these responses can be brought into balance (also known as allostasis) then two arms of the nervous system work in an integrated, cooperative manner.

The most compelling contribution of this book may be these interventions for bringing the sympathetic and parasympathetic nervous system into a harmonious working relationship. The partnership of sympathetic and parasympathetic responses is basic to handling all transitions and the myriad unexpected events of life. Empowering families to instill resources for self-regulation in their children is the key to moving forward to higher level activities and accomplishments. Lucy Jane Miller states it succinctly: "Therapies that improve self-regulation increase a child's ability to manage the fight/flight reaction and to function in situations where overreaction would hamper development." (Miller 2006, p.254) This is one of those therapies!

Flows to Balance Under Responsiveness: Parents can arouse and vitalize their child's under responsiveness in a variety of ways using simple applied touch routines. These applications, particularly in the morning when an under-responsive youngster is sluggish, can alchemize lethargy into motivation. Jump-starting adrenal function is the key.

Adrenal Wake Up: Hold the coccyx or tailbone with one hand and touch the center of the chest or middle #13 with the other hand. Then hold the top of the shoulder (#11) and the groin area on the same side (#15). Now do the same thing on the other side.

Alternately you can just use the first part of this treatment, holding the coccyx or base of the tailbone with the center of the chest (#13) as an Adrenal Wake Up. Additional options for adrenal regeneration are included in Figure 5.9.

You can use the recipe that seems most appropriate at the time or employ both, using one after the other. This will not be redundant or over-loading but you want to maintain an attuned contact

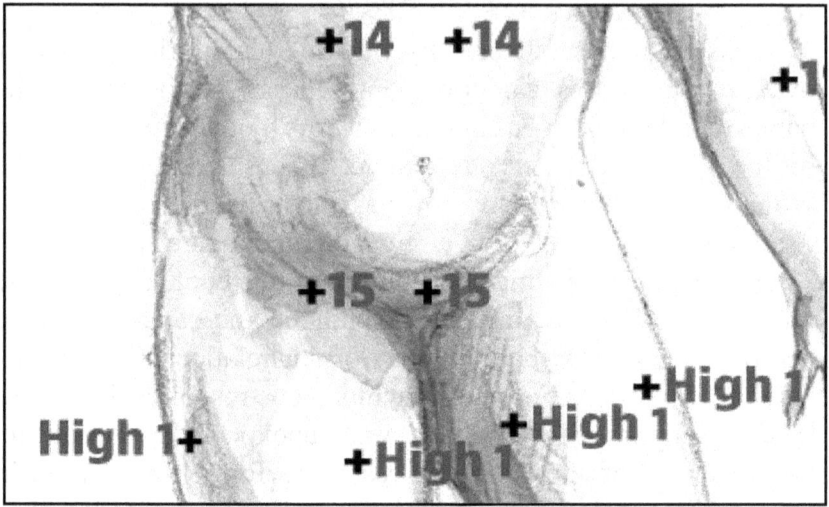

Figure 5.7 #15

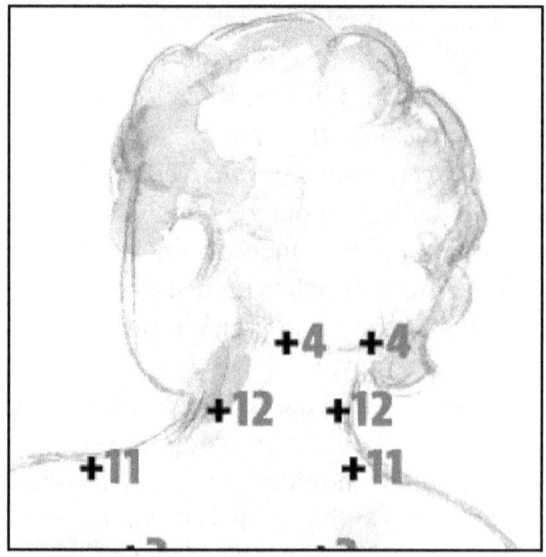

Figure 5.8 #11

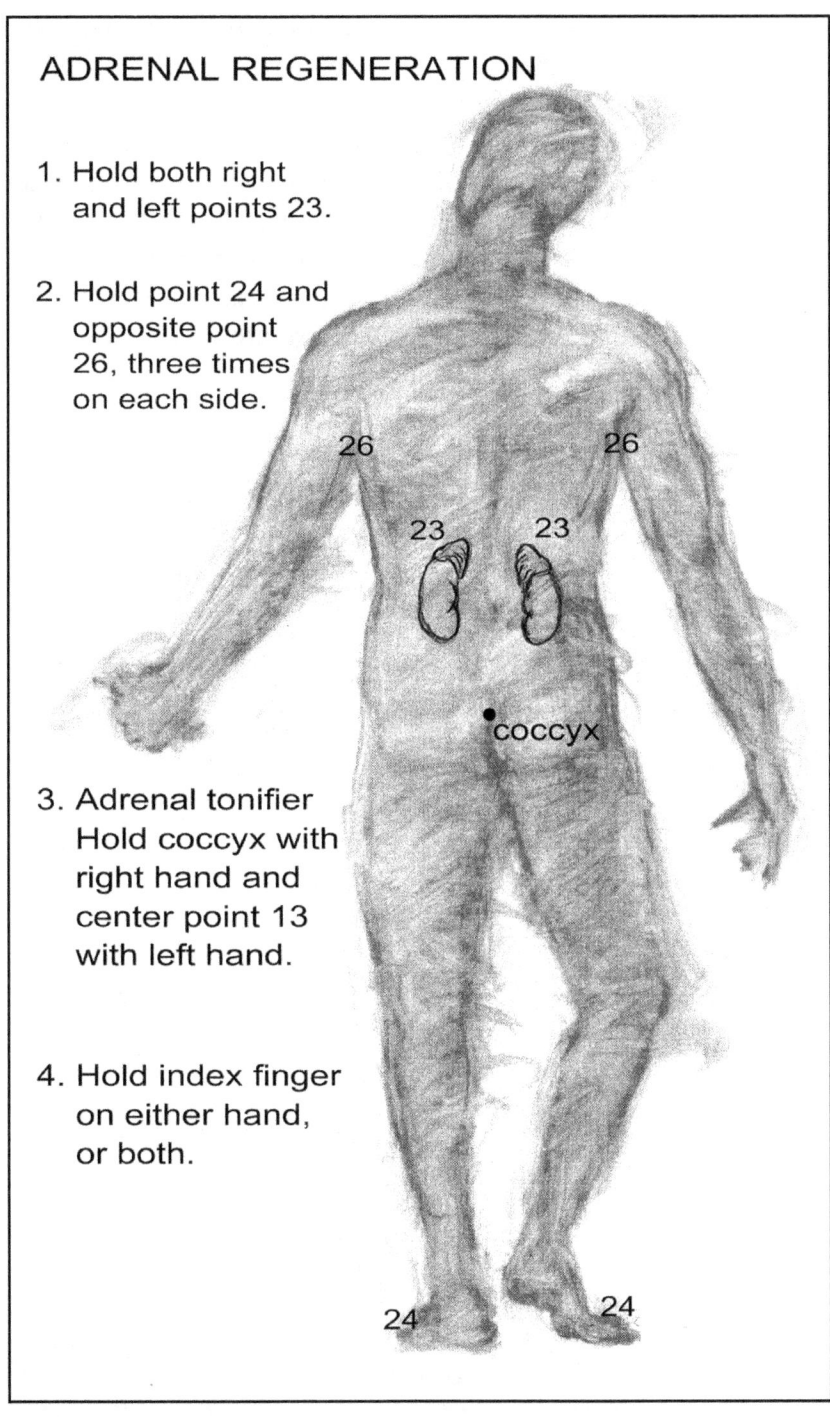

Figure 5.9 Adrenal Regeneration

New Frontiers in Sensory Integration

with the child you are treating, or who is self-treating, to monitor their responses. See the story of Daniel Dearborn in Chapter Six for additional approaches for under-responsiveness.

Flows to Balance Over Responsiveness: Parents whose children have an overly stimulated sympathetic nervous system stuck in fight and flight mode can use applied touch to calm this chaos. Simple applications used at night and first thing in the morning (or whenever over responsiveness is apparent), will re-entrain the nervous system to be less vigilant and aggressive, introducing new options for smooth functioning.

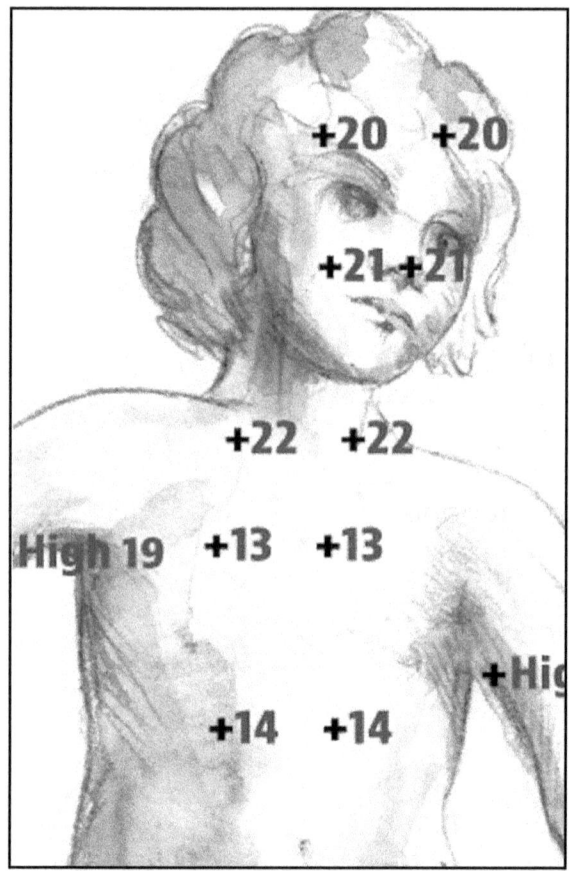

Figure 5.10 Locate middle 20 between the right left 20, on the forehead. Locate middle 14 between the right and left 14, on the midline, at the base of the sternum. These two areas can be palmed, or contacted with the palm of the hand.

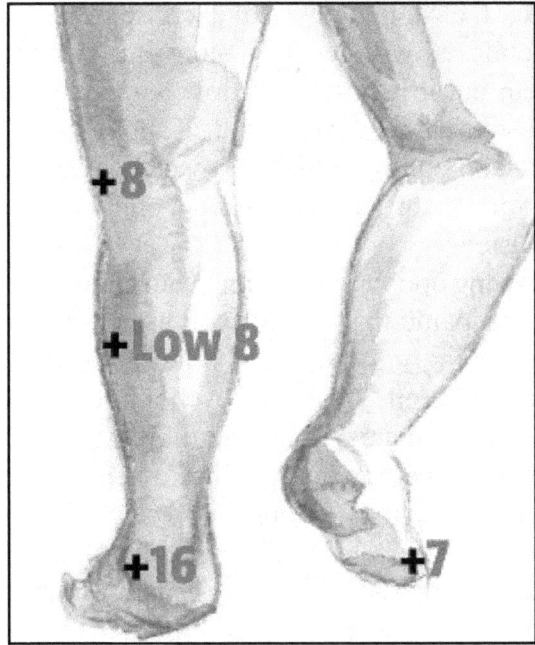

Figure 5.11 Place palm of one hand between the right and left #14 (middle 14) and with the other hand grasp both big toes holding at the base, on the sole side (#7)

Adrenal Calming: Hold the crown of the head and the center of the forehead (middle 20). Leaving one hand on the crown of the head, move the other hand to the middle of the sternum (middle 14). Finally, hold the base of both big toes (#7) with one hand (bringing the toes together) while the other hand is on the middle of the sternum (middle 14).

Melt-downs, Resistance, Confrontation and Conflict

One of the greatest challenges for parents is to push their children towards growth in areas where they are resistant or protest. Another stumbling point is handling melt-downs, especially those that include confrontation and conflict.

Putting on the hat of demanding task-master or disciplinarian is not a first choice for many parents but it is an essential component of their wardrobe. For children with low muscle tone or dyspraxia, for instance, hard work is beneficial like pushing a shopping cart, cleaning, physical exercise, walking, and working. These children will generally not want to do this. It is not easy for them but it is how they grow and have successful and satisfying lives. How can we introduce applied touch in the face of resistance and confrontation? How can we shorten the duration of melt-downs or tantrums when a child is over-stimulated or just exhausted?

The following options for calming your child's nervous system can change the panic that comes with a melt-down at a family gathering or outing into a sigh of relief after a brief interlude of treatment. Children, youth and even adults are resistant as a primal survival mechanism because they feel threatened at the introduction of the new and unfamiliar. When the adrenal system is balanced it lessens the old. outmoded sense of threat.

The Flow for Adrenal Calming provided above is soothing if a child is having a melt-down or is resistant. Obviously an active child may not allow touch, but some children are receptive to it when they are upset. More active children can be reminded to treat themselves by holding their index finger to calm the adrenals, or you can simply place your hands casually on their adrenal area (#23) without creating a treatment situation. My experience is that children want to stop their melt-downs and lessen their resistance as much as adults want them to, or perhaps even more, but they don't know how. Learning and practicing self-care when a child is calm, before the patterns of resistance and melt-down occur, and then reminding them to use applied touch when they are disturbed is effective. I have seen it work over and over again. Many children love the practices so much that they teach them to their friends at school and gain popularity because of this. When children have the experience of their nervous system changing as a result of self-care they are motivated to use these interventions when they are agitated.

Holding the Fingers

Each finger addresses one of the basic states of mind that can be the source of a melt-down or tantrum. As you hold each finger by simply wrapping the fingers of the other hand around it, you balance that attitude so that it no longer destabilizes the nervous system's equilibrium. Holding the thumb relieves worry. Holding the index finger lessens fear. Holding the middle finger calms anger. Holding the ring finger soothes sadness. Holding the little finger provides confidence and lessens over-efforting. See Figure 7.1 for an illustration of the fingers. You can also hold the palms of both hands together (as in prayer) for complete nervous system integration in one action. Children love to do all of these treatments for themselves.

One mother tells the story of her son's tantrum at a performance the family was attending. Grandma was there too and sat near the boy who was screaming and crying. Mom helped the son remember to hold his fingers and Grandma watched with amazement as the child clearly regained his composure and concentration and was able to enjoy the program with everyone else to the very end. Grandma later asked her daughter for the secret behind this remarkable magic and eventually became a student of the TARA Approach.

Figure 5.12 The Five Fingers (I gave this boy finger puppets to help him practice calming down by holding the five fingers . He relaxed so much he fell asleep!)

Another way to counter the seemingly endless distress of a melt-down is by using the prayer posture. This means simply bringing all the fingers together and pressing the palms slightly as they meet. This is called "Palm Inju" or posture.

Figure 5.13 Prayer or Palm Inju

Adults can model this on themselves when a child is having a tantrum. You will see the child simply mirror the adult. No words have to be spoken.

Palming the Calves

Palming the calves of the legs is a dependable way to calm the nervous system. This does require that the child lie down though it can be done in a seated posture. Simply place the palms of your hands on the calves of the child's legs, holding both calves simultaneously. This is always effective within less than a minute. This treatment before bedtime will assure a peaceful night's sleep. One girl who I treated with this recipe as an adolescent grew up to do a medical internship in Haiti. She sent me a letter telling me about using Palming the Calves on a patient who had surgery without anesthesia and was in agony. Within moments of receiving the applied touch treatment the patient fell into a restful slumber.

Figure 5.14 Palming the Calves

Holding the Shoulders

When a parent, care provider or therapist places their hands on the shoulders of an upset child (holding #3 and #11 on both sides), there is a cascade of relaxation that descends through the child's body. This intervention is easy to apply even for an actively

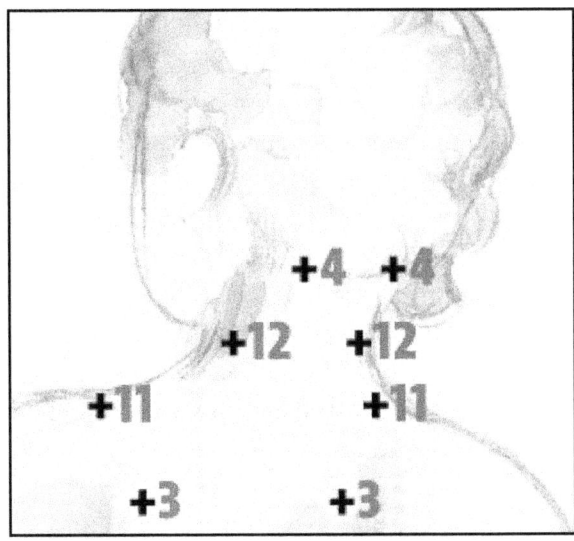

Figure 5.15 Holding #3 and #11

upset youngster or adolescent. The adult can stand or sit behind the youngster. The quality of touch can vary depending on the child's needs. Sometimes a strong, firm pressure is most effective. At other times a more casual, softer placement is needed.

Winding Down for Rest

The following two treatments (Figure 5.16 and Figure 5.17) have been clinically tested to demonstrate their capacity to help autistic children between the ages of four and eight-years-old feel calmer. So many neurodiverse children are over-efforting to find a way to be accepted or to control their bodies so that they can be more functional. They often wind up so much they completely lose the pathway to winding down. These treatments aid them by gently coaching their nervous systems to peace.

Unraveling the Causes of Stress for Sensory Integration Needs

As you unwind your stress sometimes you relax so much that you clearly see its causation. This is because the pattern of activation is interrupted. You notice you are not disturbed at moments when you previously were. You can more lucidly penetrate your children's patterns because of your enhanced awareness. Candace and Zoe's experience illustrates this. Candace wanted to enjoy theatrical events with her ten-year-old daughter Zoe, but Zoe became very agitated in these settings. Candace assumed it was because of the darkness but then she noticed that the agitation actually began in the parking lot or in the lobby. Maybe it was the movement? She tried ear phones and sunglasses en route to the theater, plus calming applied touch before getting out of the car. Bingo! Candace attributed her insight to the fact that she had been treating herself with applied touch and approached the dilemma much more gracefully, with pure curiosity rather than regret, assumptions or anxiety.

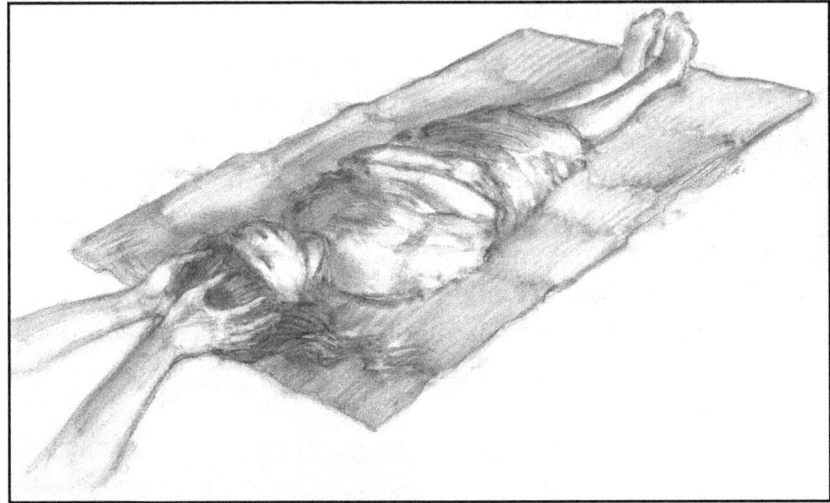

Figure 5.16 Trinity Release

Figure 5.17 11/14 Release

Using Applied Touch for Cranial Support

Children and youth with sensory integration needs are inordinately stressed. The tensions of their lives frequently result in headaches, furrowed brows and expressions of distressing confusion. Facial muscles tighten and constrict expression. The challenge of social engagement and knowing what to say and what to hold back strains the entire network of face, eyes, mouth, neck, and shoulders. Autistic children work hard in their concentrated effort to make their words, minds, bodies and needs coordinate appropriately. The strain takes a toll on the structures of the face and cranium.

When I was the parent of a young child with craniosynostosis I was empowered by learning how to do cranial treatments for her that ultimately resulted in her cranial realignment and prevented an invasive surgery. I want to pass this benefit on to others. The cranial treatments I share here are integrative, arouse resiliency and enhance the flow of cranial sacral fluid (CSF). The Trinity Release (Figure 5.16) is one of the easiest and most effective of these. It simply involves placing the palms of your hands on the crown of the child's head. Your fingers drape towards the ears. This will never overwhelm a child though you must always follow them if they wish to stop treatment.

Here are some others:

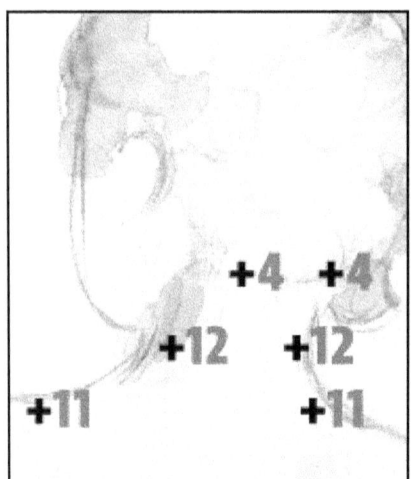

Figure 5.18 Holding Both #4's and #20's

Hold the base of the occiput (right and left #4) with the palm of one hand and let the palm of the other hand rest on the forehead (right and left #20).

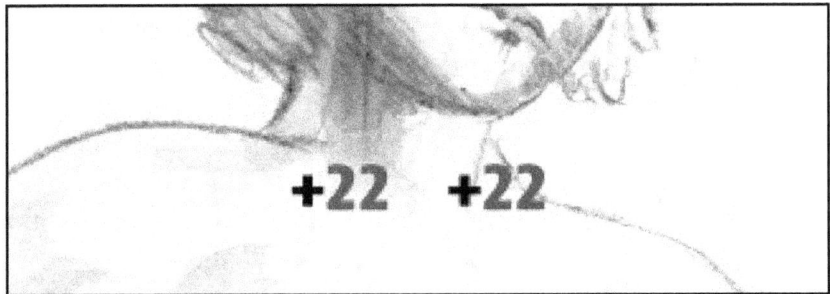

Figure 5.19 #22

Hold just under the knobby head of the collarbones (#22) on both sides simultaneously.

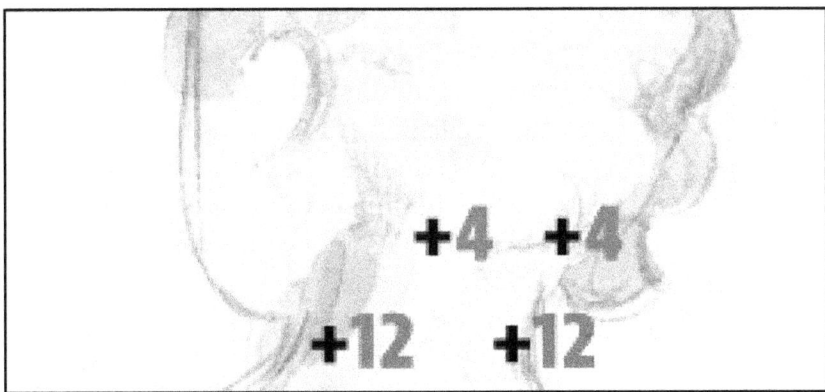

Figure 5.20 #12

Hold below the sub-occipital area (#12) on both sides simultaneously.

Summary: Pointers for Using Applied Touch
1. Applied acu-touch is a simple, non-invasive system that anyone can use effectively. Feel positive and undaunted. It is completely safe. You cannot make a mistake.
2. Your aware presence, caring and attunement qualify you to be effective and to stimulate successful, balancing responses.

3. The sites you touch are on a map of the body based on meridian lines or energy pathways. The sites are highly charged bio-electrical regions that serve specific functions.
4. This approach has been clinically tested for children with autism. Applications, including those provided in this chapter, improved behavior, social engagement and learning consistently for the subjects in the study. (Mines, Morris and Persun 2012, (in press *inter alia*)[5]. The quality of touch you employ, whether deep or soft, can be selected by the child's preferences without compromising effectiveness. The entire system is adaptable according to individual needs.
5. The length of time for treatment can also vary based on the receptivity and comfort of the child being treated.
6. Specific recipes or holding prescribed sites in particular combinations are designed for sensory needs. These treatments balance habituated nervous system firing including over and under responsiveness, defensiveness, tension, stress and agitation.
7. Applied acu-touch is a mind-body approach that promotes calm and relaxation. It can be used for all ages.
8. Parents and care-givers can implement treatments for themselves as well as for the children in their care. Indeed, adults are encouraged to first use the recipes on their own bodies so that they can feel secure about applications for children. Adults benefit from the use of this system, particularly in the relief from exhaustion and stress.
9. There is a four inch radius surrounding each site so even a general touch that encompasses that radius produces benefit. Though this system resembles acupuncture (without the needles) it is unique in this regard. Touch does not have to be precise.
10. Attunement, creativity and empathy coupled with applied touch are a potent formula for enhanced effectiveness.
11. Applied touch is effective for cranial decompression, enhancing the flow of cranial sacral fluid (CSF) and stimulating motivation and focus.

12. As the individual's nervous system finds its innate homeostasis the causes behind allostatic load or extreme stress are often revealed. This is the byproduct of relaxation that stimulates awareness without effort.
13. If you find that this system is useful and beneficial and would like to explore it further you can do so by contacting Dr. Mines and the TARA Approach through the website: www.Tara-Approach.org.

Chapter Six
The Dancing Brain: Using the Arts for Brain Resiliency

"I get up. I walk. I fall down. Meanwhile, I keep dancing."
❖ Daniel Hillel

This chapter invokes for adults the agility and creative resiliency they need to support children with sensory integration issues. When young people cannot find within themselves the sorting, organizing and filtering mechanisms to balance their sensory input they rely on the adults around them to help them develop these resources. Adult creativity must be sufficiently charged to meet this demand.

This chapter is about empowering adults to transform therapy into play. This is the essence of limbic stimulation. The arts metabolize experience and enhance the assimilation of complex sensory overload. This is why Einstein played the violin, Picasso painted and Emily Dickinson and William Butler Yeats wrote poetry. Art is an equalizer. People are united in the joys of making and experiencing art.

The art form that I spend the most time on in this chapter is story-making and its natural by-product of storytelling. These are my particular areas of expertise. I recommend that you incorporate other arts like music, movement, drawing, painting, sculpture, photography, film-making, collage and any art form with which a child resonates. The concepts that I utilize for story-making can be translated into any other art form. One child, for instance, who did not want to make a story simply drew it instead and made a visual book. Chapter Seven guides you to cultivate your capacity to use and integrate all the arts for niche construction.

Non-verbal children can participate fully in all the arts. Sophie models this. If you are skeptical about a child's receptivity to the arts I can tell you that in my recent clinical trials with autistic children between the ages of four to eight years old, all of the subjects demonstrated a marked increase in their capacity to attend to, create and develop stories while experiencing the applied touch interventions presented in this book.

The biographies of some of the world's greatest artists are models for the power of the arts to relay the brilliant and unique perceptions of the neurodiverse. In this chapter and elsewhere in this book I reference some of them to underscore the premise that the arts are apt vehicles for children to use to help them organize their rich sensory abundance. Young people enjoy hearing these biographies because they identify with them.

Welcoming Authentic Expression

All adults can learn to create safe environments to help children sort their complex sensory experiences with art. Physical activities, exercise and sports are other avenues for sorting, release and expression. Finding and implementing what best supports your child's unique development is called niche construction. Brain-to-brain resonance informed by a theory of mind conveys a reliable felt sense of safety to children in all areas of life and this is especially true when using the arts and movement. Niche construction is a true shelter for a child with sensory integration needs. It provides the motivation to grow, learn and explore the world and the people in it. When you combine your empathic presence with applied touch the results are remarkable as my research demonstrates. (Mines, Morris and Persun 2012, in press, *inter alia*)

For a child safety and trust flows from the feeling that the adults around her are paying attention and that they can participate in her kinesthetic, implicit child realms while simultaneously being responsible for the environment. Children with sensory needs thoroughly feel the absence or presence of these conditions. The adult brain is intended to be available for children to use as an instrument for their development. Children rely on this.

Adults are telling children stories about life, trust, who they are and what is possible through their behaviors and responses all the time. It is much better to be conscious of the stories you are telling children then to be unconscious of them. Adults tend to underestimate children generally and especially those who have sensory confusion. If, in contrast, you assume that there is intelligence in a young person's choices and become curious about that intelligence then you are promoting sensory integration.

The struggle for young people diagnosed with Sensory Processing Disorder is to channel their sensory abundance into comprehension and expression. The arts are containers spacious enough to accommodate the multiple strands of sensory input that weave within the brains and bodies of these youngsters. In addition, the arts demand enough structure to stabilize expression and direct it but not so much structure that sensory abundance is negated. Any adult can bring the arts into niche construction for sensory processing purposes. The education and resources you need to do that are in this book.

Mother Teresa said that "the biggest disease in this world is the feeling of being unwanted."(Teresa 2001, first published 1995, p. 94) Neurodiverse children are told by the world in countless ways, some subtle and some not so subtle, that they are not wanted as they are. The loneliness that springs from that exclusion burdens the nervous system so heavily that it impinges on development. "Most parents suppose that an authentic non-autistic self is hidden inside autistic people," says Andrew Solomon in his investigation into difference. But when parents see meaning in their child as they are, "these children have a better developmental outcome." (Solomon 2012, pp. 37, 43) Repeated rejection understandably creates fear about expression and about the world. To engage neurodiverse children in the arts we have to counter that fear with recognition and participatory modeling. The great storyteller Hans Christian Anderson who, it has been posited, suffered from severe sensory integration difficulties, grew up in abject poverty. His family was a brief shelter that encouraged his use of story making. Hans had to leave home at the age of fourteen after the death of his father but his early experiences of nourishment for his unique intelligence gave him the sense of self he needed to thrive. What a sensory needs child obsesses about may well be the key to his genius. The young Hans was over-focused on stories and used to make costumes for his characters. Rather than ridiculing him as some of his schoolmates did, his parents encouraged Hans, giving him scraps of fabric and listening to his marvelous tales. Eventually the whole world would too. Temple Grandin repeatedly reports her personal experience with the benefits of turning an obsession into a satisfying future career orientation. Here is a statement from her book *The Way I See It:*

> It is a mistake to stamp out a child's special interests, however odd they may seem at the time. In my own case, my talent in art was encouraged. My mother bought me professional art materials and a book on perspective drawing when I was in grade school. Fixations and special interests should be directed and channeled instead of abolished to make a person more 'normal'. (Grandin 2011, p.35)

Become an Artist with Your Child

When I talk to therapists and parents about using the arts they are often intimidated. The suggestion that they would speak (or paint or dance) from the heart fluidly and imaginatively with children evokes their hesitancy and embarrassment. They think this must be something I can do and they cannot. Nothing could be further from the truth. Anyone can tap the wellsprings of creativity. It is a birthright. It does, however, require a willingness to take the risk of plunging into the unknown and feeling foolish for a moment, until you relish the playfulness so much that you begin to long for it all the time! Nothing will capture the limbic attention of a child more than seeing an adult being child-like.

Recently I attended a play at a church in a small town where I was teaching at a special education program. The community did not have a big budget for their production. The adults were putting on a play for a holiday. It was a parable. Their costumes were hardly extravagant and the props were makeshift, but the actors really got into their roles. They were all adult members of the congregation with no professional acting experience, just a willingness to participate. Most of the actors were the parents, teachers and therapists for the children who live with sensory challenges who were in the program for which I was teaching. The adults were immersed in their roles and were clearly enjoying the entire event. The children could not have been more engaged if they had been at a million dollar multi-media production. Their laughter and cries of encouragement filled the room. When adults let themselves reveal the child within them then children relax and rejoice. The joys of being silly and laughing together erased any sense of difference and invited everyone into an environment of inclusion.

Getting down on the floor and playing alongside children, whether as a parent, an aide, a care provider or a therapist, provides safety. Being fully present at the child's level stimulates the limbic brain through companionable presence. The continuity of such experiences builds a sense of inclusion. Sitting behind a child and not making eye contact while he plays with a computer or a device may have other benefits but it is not a stimulant for the limbic brain and social engagement.

Stories and Art for Limbic Stimulation

My passion for the arts and particularly for story-making has been with me most of my life. Now that the neurological evidence has emerged to validate how stories and narratives are beneficial for sensory integration and bi-hemispheric resonance I am celebrating my innate intelligence and grateful for the enforcement now to share this resource for the benefit of children everywhere. As I was growing up I knew that my internal storytelling and story-making was positive. I could feel that it was stabilizing and balancing me. This has taught me to value a child's innate inclination to orient towards health. From this I have learned to follow children on their creative adventures. I wholeheartedly exhort young people with sensory challenges to tell their own stories. I invite them to write, draw, move or talk into recording devices or type. Biography is the core of inspiration and what we know best.

Autobiographical reporting in any form ends secrecy and

isolation. Our gratitude goes out to all those with sensory challenges who are courageously sharing their lives. Doing so is an act of love. We plant the seeds of this kind of love when we help children access expressive art mediums. You can easily identify the art forms that meet a child's needs. The youngster will brighten in the experience of it. This brightness is in their eyes, their skin, their language and their movement. Watch for it!

As I have been writing this book I have unveiled for myself the magnitude and the magnificence of my own sensory issues, helping me understand why I am so insistent on advocacy. Like Aaron Likens in his book *Finding Kansas*, (Likens 2012) I believe I wrote, and still write, to survive. The imagination is a spacious place. Sensory abundance calls for space. As a child I gave myself the gift of space through my imagination. I am not quite sure how I knew to alchemize my sensory abundance into internalized stories and then later into poems, books and screenplays. Yet this has given me a route to connecting with the world. It is into the expressive community of active and creative artists, innovators and visionaries that we want to welcome other burgeoning sensory abundant artists of the future. Do not hesitate to invite story-making into the lives of non-verbal children. Without exposure to language it cannot be learned. If language is not being actively stimulated then the related centers in the brain will atrophy as in any non-use. A varied, even a gourmet diet of intelligent language fed to non-verbal children will nourish their language centers.

What follows are some structures for parents and therapists to help them forge partnerships with children to foster limbic stimulation with all the arts, particularly the language arts.

Begin at the Beginning

All children love stories about themselves. When they participate in creating and telling their stories they reveal layers of feeling. Images, colors and characterization become venues to sort, filter and channel sensory experience. The role of co-participating adults is to ask engaged questions and make attuned comments to develop a collaboration in which the child is the leader. Forced, overly effusive enthusiasm is suspicious. Demonstrate that you are paying attention with respectful dialogue and inquiries. Do not be distracted. No cell phones allowed!

The First Time I Saw You Stories and Art: Telling the story of the birth of a child or the first time that child was seen in the world establishes a landmark in personhood. This is perhaps the most popular story form I use. You see variations of it throughout this book, as in the story of Sergei in Chapter Three.

Inviting a child to collaborate with you on a First Time Story using words, video, color and movement is a remarkable opportunity for limbic stimulation. This can be an interactive family experience or a therapeutic one offered by a therapist, or both. The First Time Story can be told multiple times and in many ways. It is a rite of passage.

The watershed, genre creating American writer Mark Twain (Samuel Clemens) was born prematurely and not expected to live. His biographers record his hypersensitivity, rapid cycling moods, and hair trigger nerves. His childhood was laced with repeated terror. Ron Powers, one of Twain's biographers says that these traits "have to be considered in the context of a difficult birth and the convalescence from it." (Powers 2005, p.8) Ellie's story, later in this chapter shows you see how the burdens of birth and neonatal sensory overload can be lifted from a child's nervous system through story-making and story sharing so that creativity can blossom with less stress then Mark Twain carried.

Limbic Stimulation: Using Stories for Sensory Struggles and Ritualized Behavior

Limbic stimulation requires that adults, through their attuned relationship and hemispheric resonance with children, help them de-condition habituated patterns. There are two aspects to this de-conditioning. One is engaged dialogue that can be translated to story-making to make it more playful than talk therapy. The other is the use of applied touch.

Ritualizing can be compensatory behavior initiated to control frightening and threatening sensory overload. A child may, for example, establish strict conditions about eating to feel safer. Hannah's story in Chapter Two is an illustration of this and reflects the evidence regarding prematurity and eating struggles. (Natensohn and Toomey 2012)

We are living in an unusual time in regards to children and eating. Sharp increases in the numbers of children under the age of ten with eating disorders are alarming parents and professionals worldwide. In 2010 the American Academy of Pediatrics reported a 15% increase in eating disorders of various kinds since 2003, but what is striking is that the largest number was amongst patients younger than seven years old. (American Academy of Pediatrics 2010)

According to Abigail Natensohn, author of *Feeding Disorders and Picky Eating in Infants and Children,* one out of every twenty children in the US between the ages of birth and ten years refuses to eat or will only eat limited amounts of selected foods. (Natenshon and Toomey 2012, p.134) Difficulties with eating are often partnered with sensory processing disorders, including Asperger's, Pervasive Developmental Disorders, Non-verbal Learning Disability and Autism. Clinical trials are being conducted now to investigate this correlation. (Ianco, Cohen, Yehuda and Kotler 2006, pp. 189-193) The leading charity serving the disordered eating population in the UK reported in 2011 that eating problems were on the rise for children under the age of twelve. (B-eat 2010)

Asking a child why they don't eat or why they refuse certain foods is usually unproductive. Children cannot generally answer that question. Adults have to be more creative in their inquiries. We can reflect deeply about the child's experience and history and observe them to see into the mystery of their sensory struggles with eating. When we enter their world and meet them dynamically where they are we can make breakthroughs. The time we need for this reflection is hard won I know, but well worth it.

Ellie's story, like Hannah's in Chapter Two, illustrates the process of using creativity to address the sensory struggles surrounding ritualizing food and eating. The strategy of making the sensory needs child the star of the story is almost always successful with younger children. All the stories in this chapter are models for any sensory driven ritualized behavior. Using the child's name and aspects of her history can be an effective strategy. Ellie ritualistically avoided certain foods and became rigid and withdrawn in any eating environment. Her learning was delayed and she struggled with comprehension and focus. She withdrew from challenges readily. Ellie's birth weight and APGAR scores were alarmingly low. This was pertinent information because it explained the way that vulnerability and isolation were coupled for her. Her parents agreed to try a story-making and storytelling approach to incorporate the impacts of her early history on her sensory patterns.

The story we told Ellie was about her birth and immediate post-natal experience. It became known later as the story of when Ellie came to dinner because that is what she did after she heard the story. Ellie was nine years old when her parents and I told her this story but her behavior, understanding and language processing was more like that of a much younger child.

Once upon a time there was a newborn baby girl named Ellie," the story begins.

Ellie was so little she had to live in a special place before her Mommy could hold her.

Her Mommy and Daddy named her Eleanor because that means little shining light but they called her Ellie for short.

In Ellie's special place there was always a light shining on her to keep her warm.

Every day Ellie's Mommy and Daddy sat by her side in the special place and said, "You are our little shining light."

One day Ellie opened her eyes and looked right into her Mommy's eyes.

Her Mom smiled at her and said, "You made it! I am so proud of you."

After this Ellie could come out of her special place and her Mommy and Daddy held her and hugged her. Her Mommy could feed her now right from her body!

The three of them were happy to be together.

From that day on Ellie could eat and sleep at home with everyone around her, including her brother and sister.

She got bigger and bigger but her Mommy and Daddy still called her their little shining light.

After I told her this simple story Ellie stayed on the couch where she was sitting close to her dad, resting on his lap. I guided her dad to use applied touch to help Ellie integrate this reframing of her early experience from threatening to welcoming. Her dad placed his hands softly around Ellie. One hand rested just above her waist in the small of her back (# 23). The other hand was on the opposite side of her back, behind her arm pit (#26). His hands felt warm. After a while he moved his hands so that they were holding the same places but on the opposite sides of her back. Ellie's head rested comfortably on his chest and her legs dangled across his lap. She could lean on him but she also felt like he was holding her.

When the family went to the dinner table that evening, Ellie joined them quite naturally, as if it were completely familiar. In truth, this was something she had not done without argument and coaxing for a long time. Such a straightforward gesture, taken for granted in many homes, was felt as a blessing in her home that evening. The story memorialized her tender transformation.

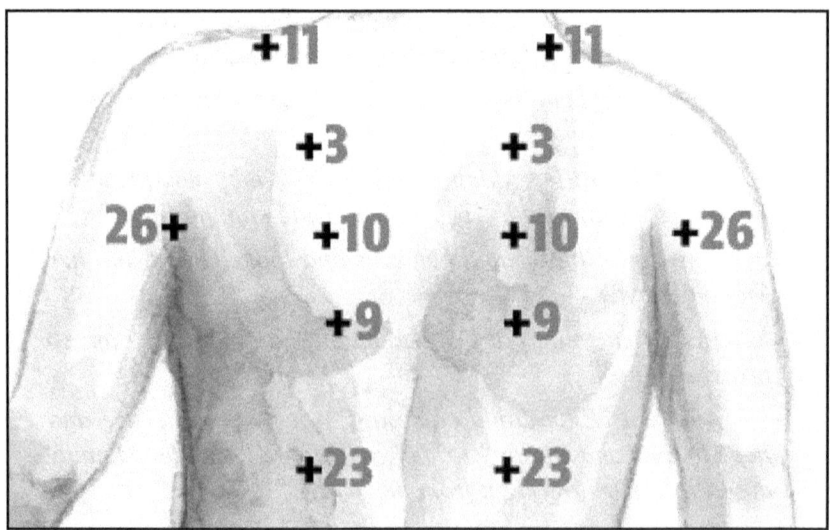

Figure 6.1 #23 and #26

Every Day is a Work of Art

Another accessible story template that is effective for helping young people with sensory integration is to tell the story of their day. This can be an excellent bed time story because it provides an opportunity to highlight accomplishments leading to peaceful satisfied sleep.

Prioritizing the positive supports the allostasis or homeostasis of the nervous system. You can tell the story of a triumph over any difficulty, no matter how small, or you can turn mundane events into a celebration. As parents and care-givers make stories for and with children they cultivate the neurology of self-affirmation.

The vignette that follows comes from my experiences with Lou Anne who was diagnosed with PDD-NOS (Pervasive Developmental Disorder Not Otherwise Specified). Lou Anne was a dominantly non-verbal young lady but she periodically used language spontaneously. She was quite withdrawn, shy and parasympathetic. The story about Lou Anne that I created for her supports and reflects her improving proprioception and increasing physical strength. Prior to the event that is retold in the story Lou Anne had rarely acted independently of her mother. Color and feeling are included to enhance Lou Anne's sensory integration. If you tell a story to a non-verbal child be sure to have art supplies at hand and invite her to express her responses using them. I was so struck by the gains for Lou Anne encapsulated in this story that I audio recorded it for her ongoing benefit as well as inviting her to illustrate it. It is of priceless value to landmark gains for children who struggle with sensory integration. Their daily lives often feel like reiterations of their difficulties. Countering that with the opposite is essential. Stories can be used to establish milestones in emotional memory and build limbic bridges to higher cognition.

If you record or write a story using any media that is available, it can be retold whenever a boost is needed. A story like this can be illustrated, printed and even filmed.

The Day Lou Anne Said YES!

Once there was a girl named Lou Anne who liked to ride her red bicycle and feel the cool handlebars on her soft, warm hands. She planted her feet firmly on the bike pedals. Her shoes had green neon stripes that caught her eye when she looked down. She felt steady in her strong shoes. Lou Anne's bicycle was her friend but she always went on adventures with her mom, her other best friend. One day her brother Gavin invited her on an adventure. He wanted to go to the store to buy a treat. He had earned the money and he wanted to share it with his sister. Gavin was a great big brother but Lou Anne wasn't too sure about this. Then Lou Anne noticed that she had on her coolest bright pink bike shorts and her pink striped hat and she just said YES, out loud.

The air felt gentle as it moved through her curly hair on the way to the store. Gavin helped Lou Anne lock her bike outside and he let her push the cart in the store. They bought the makings for strawberry lemonade and chocolate chip cookies and carried them in their bicycle baskets. Gavin carried the lemonade and Lou Anne carried the cookies. . When they got home their mother was waiting for them. "Did you have a good time?" she asked. Lou Anne answered clearly and loudly, with her favorite word, "Yes!"

Lou Anne collaborated with me on this story using her computer and yes/no switches. Her facial expressions and occasional utterances also played a part in the making of this story. When a child sees or hears their own experience mirrored back to them it changes their brain. Their evolutionary potential increases by an order of magnitude. This is why I recommend short biographical stories or vignettes to prioritize positive growth for a child with sensory processing difficulties.

After this story making experience and the sharing of the story with her family Lou Anne took more independent action. She had a positive reference point for considering activities with others. She always would need a trusted advocate and speaker like her brother, but there were others who could do this for and with her in her community. This gave her mother much needed respite that was long overdue and expanded Lou Anne's world. Because her own articulation had been safe and supported, she was more confident about future utterances.

I Used to Be and Now I Am: This is a biography story in which the focus is on growth and achievement, this time reflecting on a change like "I used to be shy to speak and now I say hello to my friend," or "It used to be hard to tie my shoes and now it's not. I can do it!" You can make a collection of these comparative statements and make stories based on progress and achievements. The rhythm and similarity of word use and patterns of phrasing will be appealing to the children who enjoy repetition. They can entrain to positive repetitions that reflect their accomplishments.

For older youth you can make the story-making and storytelling casual and conversational by reflecting with them on their development. You can say things like, "Look at you! You totally shifted how angry you were at that teacher and changed your behavior. You worked hard to do that! You can do that now. Wow. You go!" Follow this with a high five or any other connective and validating gesture and you have a mini version of the upgraded I Used to Be and Now I Am storyline for sensory development.

Global Sensory Overload and Pacing Interventions

Here are the words of a young adult with sensory processing difficulties who, upon reflection on his childhood, recognized how his enormous receptivity to everything and everyone around him so overwhelmed his nervous system that he felt he had no option but to withdraw. Labeled as a bashful, retiring loner, he was actually longing to be in contact with others but did not have a clue how to come out of the confusion of global sensory overload.

> *"I could walk into a room and feel what everyone is feeling. The problem is that it all came in faster than I could process it. So I behaved as if I was disconnected when I was really too connected."*

A child may be withdrawn and unable to navigate in a play environment because of being flooded by sensory messages. This is also true for neurodiverse youth in social settings. Applied touch can jump start a latent capacity to allow the likelihood of choosing to move and connect in play and with others. Use the interventions for under-responsiveness that can stimulate clarity and upload sorting mechanisms to engage more readily.

Withdrawal is a dominantly parasympathetic response to global sensory overload. Brief, biographically oriented stories can interrupt this habituated flooding and open windows of opportunity for connection. When the child is the center of the story and they feel mirrored in a positive way the shame or sense of inadequacy is muted or dissolved. This can happen implicitly for younger children and more cognitively for youth.

"Daniel Dearborn Finds His Home in His Body" provides a simple applied touch intervention (holding the top of the shoulder or #11 with the base of the sit bone or #25 on the same side) embedded within a story. As the adult tells the story, he demonstrates this treatment. While this application may at first seem mysterious or simplistic, it is based on clinically tested scientific principles that have been shown to be effective in promoting learning, presence and social engagement for autistic children. (Mines, Morris and Persun 2012, *inter alia*, in press.)

No child wants to feel separate from the community of his peers. Participatory play is an organic and essential aspect of childhood. Alleviating the burden of difference and isolation allows the child to grow socially and academically. Participation is a crucial aspect of learning and neurological development.

Feel free to use this story for any child who you notice is withdrawn from participation with others. If the child responds positively then you can explore the cause of global sensory overload further. Use the story to practice the relieving intervention repeatedly and watch to see how the child's behavior changes in response.

Daniel Dearborn Finds His Home in His Body

Once there was a boy named Daniel who knew he was different. He wanted to be part of things but he didn't know how. He was confused.

One day Daniel learned how to share. His friend Mary who helped him with Occupational Therapy showed him something he could do to feel better. She placed one of her hands on the top of her shoulder and the other hand under where she was sitting. Both hands were on the same side of her body. Then she asked Daniel to do the same thing for himself. He imitated her.

"Just see what happens when you hold these two places," Mary said. "And when you want to change to the other side you can."

When Daniel walked back to his classroom he did not feel confused. He could feel his feet inside his sneakers touching the hallway floor. When he got home he tried what he had learned again and then decided to show it to his mom. She tried it too. She liked it so much she gave Daniel a hug.

Figure 6.2 Holding #11 and #25

Sensory Integration, Vision and Reading

The story that follows about a girl named Cecelia who struggled with reading reminds me of when my daughter Rachel was five and refused to read. She threw shattering temper tantrums when it came to reading. One day in exhaustion and frustration I went for a hike in the open space by my house. I must have looked utterly distraught because a neighbor who I barely knew stopped me on the trail and asked me what was wrong. "Your daughter will read," she said with calm assurance after I explained my dilemma. "Trust her." These words were like balm to my mother's troubled heart. I took them in.

Rachel's struggle with reading was one of the first signs of what would later prove to be a variety of learning challenges, none of which were easily "visible." In testing she always fell through the cracks. Rachel did learn to read as the woman on the trail predicted, and it did also turn out that she had vision anomalies including rare astigmatisms.

Eye problems are closely correlated with cranial development at all the crucial stages including prenatally and at birth. It is difficult if not impossible for young children to articulate their vision problems. They rely on the adults around them to investigate why they may be straining to see and read. Central and/or peripheral vision anomalies may be part of the picture.

The way in which a child (or anyone) is told by a practitioner, medical professional, teacher or therapist that help is needed dramatically impacts their progress. Criticism or blaming for behavior when there are sensory processing difficulties is a shock to a child's nervous system and has multiple reverberations across time. No child or parent is guilty of having caused a sensory disorder. Reading, spelling, movement and vision problems result from a complex assortment of structural, neurological, developmental, emotional and relational issues. Relaxing the eyes is a key to higher quality vision and reading comprehension. Learning to help a child feel at peace helps their vision. Listening to stories read aloud relaxes the eyes as the child sees imaginatively from within and does not use their eye muscles. See Chapter Seven for more information and resources for vision therapies and Alex's story in Chapter Eight.

When therapists and parents try to problem solve a child's learning challenges as advocates for that child they are supporting the child's innate health. As Karen Lowry (mother of a sensory challenged child and also a parent educator and healthcare provider) points out in her excellent book, *Seventh Inning Sit,* even those trained in Special Education or who are therapists can misread, misinterpret or misdiagnose your child. Parents have to be their own self-referencing, educated authorities to advocate. They also have to follow their intimate knowledge of their child. Karen developed this wisdom from her experience advocating for her son, "Be courageous and go forward to find all the complete answers to your child's struggles. Chances are that you will be surprised at your intuitiveness." (Lowry 2008, p. 21) I highly recommend her book to all parents struggling with recalcitrant or unresponsive school systems.

You will save money and unnecessary heartache when you inform yourself and put your child in the center of the healing process. I wrote this story with CeCe and her mother to document their experience. We wanted other children, parents and therapists to hear it. Everything you need to know is in the story.

The Dancing Alphabet

Once there was a girl named Cecelia (CeCe for short) who loved to watch words dance. The letters did not stay still long enough to spell anything but they were so much fun to watch.

But her teacher at school was not happy about this. She said CeCe couldn't read.

When her mom heard what the teacher said, she replied, "But CeCe is so smart."

"Have you ever had your eyes checked?" CeCe's Grandma asked.

The eye doctor taught CeCe games so that she could learn how to hold the letters in place. CeCe got to be so good at reading and writing that she wrote this poem.

Words Play
Words play
Every day
Together
Forever.
What do they say?
"Solve the mystery.
Climb the word tree.

> Jump for joy.
> Every girl and boy
> Can read!
> It's easy,
> It's free
> When we see,
> You and me.

Interactive Stories for Social Engagement and Language Processing

As you probably have noticed many of our stories begin with "Once there was a (boy or girl) named (insert name of child)." Once you say the child's name in a story told out loud it is as if the sun comes out in their eyes. Every child loves to hear their name as the star of the story and you can trust that they will pay attention to it from that moment on. Interactive stories encourage language processing that is cadenced and balanced. You engage by asking the child to complete a story with you. If the child is reluctant recruit a parent or other adult who is present, or a sibling, into the story-making. It might go something like this:

You say: Once there was a boy named Angus and one day he...
Angus: Saw a movie about a warrior!
Then you say: And when he saw that movie he felt....
Angus: Scared.
Then you say: And when he felt scared he...
Angus: Squeezed his eyes shut!
Then you say: And when he squeezed his eyes shut he saw the color....
Angus: RED!
Then you can ask Angus to draw a picture of his feeling.

Interactive Stories for Older Children

Interactive stories for older children can be geared toward a specific obstacle that a child is facing. Writing the story becomes a route to problem solving as well as language processing and sorting emotions to deflect sensory overload. Aila was nine years old when we created this story. She wanted her real name to be used. We had seen each other frequently throughout her development so we had a comfortable relationship. We collaborated on the following story over a period of weeks that culminated in her birthday. She also illustrated the story. The entire process became like a rite of passage.

Alia lived in the midst of nature in rural Hawaii. Everything around her was lush and she spent a lot of time outdoors. At this time Alia was studying Greek mythology in her class and she was fascinated with the Goddess Mnemosyne (pronounced NEM-O-ZINE), the Goddess of Memory so she wanted to bring her into the story.

Aila told me that she was overwhelmed with feelings she did not understand when she was at school. It did not happen any other time. She felt anxiety every morning as she got ready for school. Once there her mood could change all of a sudden. One minute she would be happy and the next moment she would be sad for no reason. How did this happen? She couldn't figure it out! Here is the story we created together to help Aila overcome the obstacle of her hyper-sensitivity to others.

Aila and Mnemosyne

Once there was a girl named Aila. When Aila was at school her world would change suddenly. She felt like she was on a roller coaster of feelings. One day after school she went to a special place that she loved in the forest by her house. Aila took a deep breath when she got to this place. She felt better just being there.

Then Aila heard a voice calling her name. She looked around. She saw a tall tree with a big knothole. She went closer and looked into the hole. There was a "whoosh" and it seemed like something flew out of the hole! Aila looked down. There on the ground before her in the green grass was a beautiful fairy with iridescent wings and sparkling eyes.

"Who are you?" Aila asked.

"I am Mnemosyne," was the answer.

Aila was amazed.

"Come back tomorrow at the same time," Mnemosyne continued, "and I will be waiting."

After school the next day Aila went back to the tree. She stood in front of the knothole and called, "Mnemosyne, Mnemosyne." There was a whoosh of air as the fairy flew out.

"How was your day at school?" the fairy asked, her eyes twinkling and her wings shining.

Aila told her about how she felt confused with her feelings, like she was on a roller coaster.

"When you are in school tomorrow," Mnemosyne said, "Return all your confused feelings to wherever they came from. It's easy. Just command them to go home."

Figure 6.3 Give Yourself a Hug (hold #26 on both the right and left sides, wrapping your arms around yourself).

With that the fairy whooshed past Aila's face and flew back into the knothole. Aila went home and had a nice dinner with her family and slept very well. The next morning she arose bright and early and went to school.

At school Aila did what Mnemosyne said and after school she rushed back to the tree and called the fairy's name. Mnemosyne came out so fast she almost crashed into Aila. "How was school today?" she asked, and Aila told her about everything. She felt light and happy. The confusing feelings were gone.

But then she got worried. "How can I stay this way?" she asked Mnemosyne.

"Oh, that's easy," the beautiful fairy replied. "Just wrap your arms around yourself to give yourself a big hug." The fairy showed Aila how to do this by putting her fingertips just behind her armpits, with her arms crossed over her chest.

"How do you feel now?" asked Mnemosyne.

"I feel peaceful and happy," Aila answered with a big smile on her face. "But can I come back to talk to you?"

"You can come back any time," the bright fairy answered. "Just give yourself a hug and I will be there."

And with that Mnemosyne flew up with the whoosh of her wings, winked at Aila and flew in the knothole.

Katya, another young lady somewhat older than Alia, created very different stories to resolve her experience of sensory overload in social or public environments. Her stories were about battles between warriors with super-powers struggling to find safety from invading forces. Whatever form or content is needed to externalize difficulty so that it can be conveyed to others and shared relieves the burden of stress. Having fun being creative doing this makes it a viable therapy.

Embodiment

Aubrey, like Sophie, is someone who I have had the privilege to follow from childhood into adolescence and adulthood. I have seen how these brilliant young people step into fulfilling lives and manage their difficulties using the interventions in this book and especially the hands-on applied touch recipes that stand them in good stead. Notably Sophie and Aubrey have been able to cultivate authentic relationships that enrich their lives and the lives of their friends and family members. They have entered the world and are making contributions there as whole, engaged individuals. They change the environments they enter just as they are changing. They are co-evolving in a world that is reciprocal and responsive.

One of their biggest challenges is embodiment. Because their bodies seem to be the problem they search for other places to put their attention. Their bodies just do not behave the way they want them to and in social encounters this can be horrifying for them. They become angry with themselves and that anger can explode unexpectedly and uncontrollably.

At fifteen years Aubrey had normal social ambitions but his marked stutter got in the way. It was a complex adjunct to his autism and he hated it. I had been part of Aubrey's therapy team since he was seven years old. His pattern was to avoid his difficulties and regress. I saw this as a fear of moving forward based on his distrust and rejection of his body's ability to support him. From the standpoint of community Aubrey had it all. His parents and extended family were unified in their faith in him. His therapy team was collaborative and on point.

Aubrey had a reputation for lashing out, sometimes violently. This was his Achilles heel. His parents were concerned about what happened to Aubrey in social settings where the pressure was amped up for him in his teenage years. They wondered if he could remain in the same school with his fabulous academic mentors but where his behavioral patterns were out of bounds.

I had a meeting with Aubrey as this subject was reaching a climax.

"What do you feel in your body," I asked him, "just before you get angry? Can you see yourself at that time and look inside your body. What is happening there?"

"I am going to explode," Aubrey replied his eyes squeezed shut to illustrate his intensity.

"I can't stand it anymore," he continued. "I need to blow up."

"What would happen if you didn't?" I inquired. "Let's imagine that the explosion is bright red and it gets redder and redder. It needs to spread out. It is so red and so hot because it is squeezed into too small a space like an electrical storm in a small room."

Aubrey looked interested and curious. He was clearly trying to imagine an electrical storm confined to a room. This was compelling for him and he was focused on the details of how to make this possible.

"We can help that electricity to spread out. We can give it more space and then it won't have to strike anyone and hurt them," I went on, glad to have his interest. I knew that I had to capitalize on it when it was available.

"How?" he asked. He was definitely intrigued.

"There are some places you can hold on your body that will spread out the electricity," I answered.

"Oh, like we did before to help me speak more slowly." He smiled in recognition.

"Exactly," I replied.

I showed Aubrey #14, under the ribs on the front of the body (see Figure 5.10), by holding them on myself on both the right and left sides. I placed the palms of my hands on the two areas. He mirrored me.

"When you hold these places," I continued, building on our momentum, "Imagine that you are lifting up a window to let the electrical storm out. Can you feel the electricity changing in your body?"

Aubrey concentrated. He had done things like this before and his parents and teachers encouraged him so he was willing.

"Yes," he said, and nodded.

Over the next few weeks I got reports from Aubrey's parents and teachers that he was using the "window for the storm" application and it was working. This meant that Aubrey's interactions with his peers could last longer than five minutes, though he sometimes had to take breaks to "open the window." I was not using a story per se to help Aubrey with social engagement because I don't think a fifteen-year-old, autistic or neurotypical, wants to be told a story. Our exchange used story components, however, like metaphor and dialogue. At an earlier time in his life Aubrey might not have been responsive to metaphor but he had evolved so that metaphor was actually a component of his experience and he used it in some of his computer game programs that were designed to develop his focus.

As Aubrey continued to develop and become a young adult social relationships were always his edge. He is now in college studying computer science and is cultivating more and more genuine, reciprocal relationships. He continues to need help and consults me, on his own now and sometimes via Skype, for tools to help him manage, explore and constructively transform his unproductive responses.

Mentoring Stories

The stories of successful neurodiverse artists and scientists make excellent models to inspire children and youth. Some of these are available in published form or on videos. Parents and therapists can also collaborate with children to create their own versions from biographies they find. I refer to some of these mentors throughout this book like Hans Christian Anderson, Mark Twain, Temple Grandin, Daniel Tammet, Dawn Prince Hughes and others.

Qualities of the Storyteller

When telling or reading stories to children limbic stimulation is supported when the storytellers engage in their roles and exhibit some of the following characteristics.

The Storyteller's Gifts

"The true source of a story is in the preverbal images in the mind."
  ❖ Robin Moore, Awakening the Hidden Storyteller
  (Moore 1991, p. 19)

- Spontaneity
- Playfulness
- Cultural and Ethnic Sensitivity

- Respect
- Language: The Storyteller Translates Pictures into Words
- Expressiveness: The Storyteller Uses Expression as Language
- Humor
- Attunement
- While Being Spontaneous and Integrative, the Storyteller Stays on Track and Moves Forward
- Imagination
- Joyful in Connected Performance
- Authenticity
- Vitality
- Shared Enjoyment
- Presence
- Appropriate Eye Contact
- Strong and Confident Voice
- Playful Voice Changes
- Pacing
- Co-Participatory Engagement
- Trust in the Listener's Intelligence

Talking About Stories after You Hear or Tell Them: A child's emotional vocabulary cannot be built unless the adults around her uses an emotional vocabulary. After engaging in story-making or storytelling share your experience and inquire about the child's. Adults frequently talk in baby talk to children, whether they are neurodiverse or not. I recommend never doing this. Always talk to children intelligently and invite them to ask you about the words you use. You can also inquire from them to be sure they are understanding you and take your time explaining whatever words they are not sure about. Adjust your conversation to the age and capacity of the young person with whom you are sharing. For older youth you can condense this conversational interlude to a summary that is reciprocated by their validation. This is the nuanced affirmation that your intervention has been successful. When you get this response from an adolescent, it is a real coup.

Summary: Counter the Assault on Childhood and Natural Development through Storytelling and Communication

Stories keep childhood alive. Whether the child you serve is a patient, client or family member and whether that child is neurodiverse or neurotypical, they are barraged by the materialization of childhood that pervades modern culture. This includes a stylization of the images of childhood, obsession with technological gadgets, limited exposure to the natural world outdoors, and removal from an extended family, like grandparents and other mentors who convey hands-on skills and nature based immersions. We need to understand the implications of these developments from the child's perspective. We can't turn time backwards but we can claim the right for a child to be a child and instill practices that guarantee it.

Stories restore and speak to the undying need we all have for the magic of childhood and natural, healthy development. We allow the light of that time to fade at our own risk. Because I know and have tested the power of story- making and storytelling to invite the brain to dance I want to inspire adults to use this exquisite non-pharmaceutical medicine that is completely free of charge. There is an investment of time and focus, but this is completely worthwhile. The capacity to make stories tailored specifically for the young people in your life will stand you in good stead. When the power is down, when children are having a melt-down, when you can't go anywhere or buy anything, when the gadgets don't work and someone is agitated or cannot sleep, stories fill the void, calm the nervous system, and ease you into peace.

Chapter Seven
Cultivating Niche Construction for Sensory Integration

The basement of the house where Sophie lives is a cozy wonderland. In the winter the fireplace burns brightly. A treatment table for Sophie's applied touch sessions is set up near the warmth.. A small trampoline and a treadmill are available for movement opportunities. Brightly colored balls of different shapes, sizes and textures are nestled in a corner cube not far from the blue semi-circular art table that holds Sophie's eye gaze device, computer, art supplies and music. Baskets are full to the brim with beads, gold, and green and purple, and others that look like seeds or gourds. Cathy, Sophie's mom, has an eye for what stimulates and soothes the senses and the mind. She makes her choices based on what her daughter finds compelling and engaging. This is niche construction.

The term "niche construction" is borrowed from biology, It refers to how any organism changes its environment, usually to improve its chances of survival. Interestingly, these changes tend to reflexively enhance the environment where they occur, stimulating a co-evolutionary shift. In some cases this co-evolution can have epigenetic implications.

Cathy actively uses niche construction tools with Sophie and invites others to join in. Neighborhood children or friends from school come over to play with Sophie in her wonderland and talk to her using her eye gaze computer that they all find fascinating. Visits with Sophie are special gifts to them and unlike any other play dates.

The niche construction items that Cathy has assembled are experiential but she also has found enhancing therapeutic aids that increase Sophie's ability to be functional in life and enjoy her movement. Experiential Resources include the arts, expression and communication, and physical activities. Enhancement Resources are more clearly adjunctive therapies and therapeutic aids though sometimes the two categories blend. In both categories the criteria of empowerment is uppermost in determining Cathy's selections.

As we survey the options for niche construction, consider the neurodiverse children you serve and how their potential could be optimized by this abundance of experiential and enhancement resources.

Art: The Visual Dimensions and the World of Color

"The line between profound talent and profound disability is a surprisingly thin one." (Tammet)
❖ Daniel Tammet (in an interview)

If you observe children making art you see how they are kinesthetically drawn to it. This includes neurodiverse children and youth. Children's art mirrors their growth. You do not have to be an art therapist to use art with a child though Sophie's mom might well have earned an honorary art therapist's credential given her years of adapting the arts for her daughter. Children make sense of their world through their art. Children with sensory needs are almost constantly being "normalized" to assimilate with the neurotypical world. With art they can be free of this imposition. If a child is having difficulty recognizing emotion you can provide a "feelings guide" such as the one we provide in the Chart of the Fingers or create your own. Ask your child to draw faces or use colors and shapes to reflect the feelings on the guide and invite her to add to those feelings using art.

Art Therapy is a recognized adjunctive therapeutic approach in which art is linked with a psychotherapeutic and developmental process. This is distinct from using art for communication and expression though of course there is an overlap. The American Art Therapy Association has joined with the Autism Society of

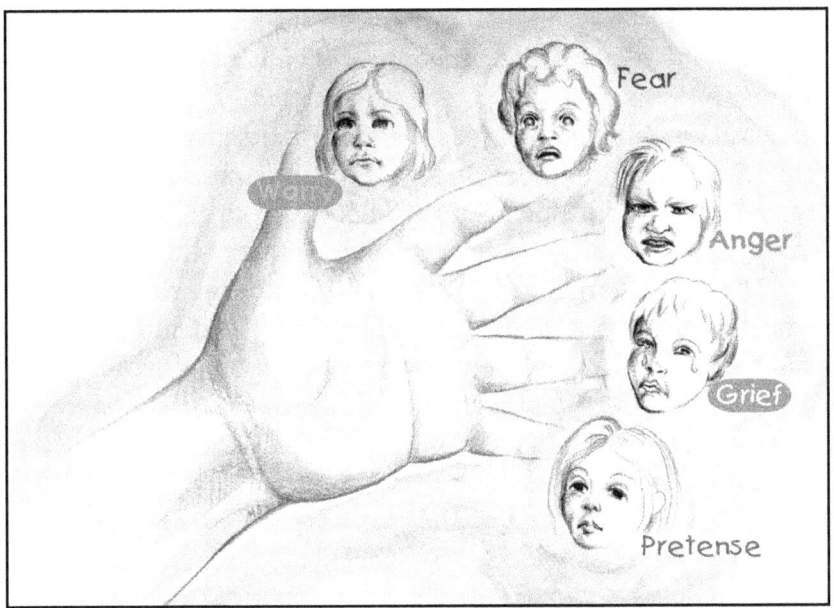

Figure 7.1 The Story of the Fingers

America to develop a tool kit for integrating creative interventions in the class room. "Art therapy ...may serve as a path towards increased awareness of the self. The sense of self is a cornerstone for relating." (Emery 2004, p. 147)

The Arts Dyslexia Trust is a UK based non-profit organization that draws attention to the creative gifts of people who are visual-spatial learners rather than primarily verbal learners. It promotes research and learning opportunities using the arts for dyslexics. It also displays their art so that others have an opportunity to view it. It helps educators understand how to integrate the arts into classroom environments to include visual-spatial learners. It helps educate parents so that they can recognize a child's learning struggles and use the arts when linear language is not working.

In Art Therapist Melissa Emery's research she notes that language development can be an outgrowth of the use of art. She emphasizes the centrality of the parents' involvement in this regard. "Parents remain key," she comments. "Their constancy is fundamental for growth and development." (Emery 2004, p.147)

You may well see that a neurodiverse child builds a strong connection with their art. Encourage this by suggesting art as a coping aid when the child is confused, sad or angry. Make art materials available wherever you go. Find sensory friendly art environments for the development of giftedness whenever you can. When an adult spends time reflecting on a child's art it contributes to cultivating theory of mind for that child.

The life and art of Richard Wawro is a striking example of the relationship between autism and art and the role of attuned parents and clinicians. Richard Wawro was a remarkable Scottish artist who earned widespread acclaim for his detailed drawings created with wax oil crayons. You can watch a YouTube video produced by autism educator Laurence Becker called *With Eyes Wide Open* that provides a glimpse into the creativity and home life of Richard Wawro. (Becker 1983) His special education teacher Molly Leishman talks about her life changing experience of introducing Richard to art with crayons in her classroom when he was six years old. All she did was notice and nurture Richard's interest in light: "I noticed that Richard became interested and attracted to moving or flickering light," she says. "This was something I felt I could use in my search for an occupation for this restless little lad ... One day I pinned paper to his desk and taking a large red wax crayon, I scribbled a few lines. He was interested....It was difficult to describe the emergence of the first picture: so unexpected it was. What I saw was magic." (Leishman 1958).

Molly Leishman and Richard's parents did not have access to advanced technology or fancy art materials. They just had their love and faith, attention, paper and crayons. Richard's first show in Edinburgh when he was seventeen was opened by Lady Margaret Thatcher who, along with Pope Paul II became a collector of Richard's art. Richard did not speak until the age of eleven and was considered severely autistic and retarded. He required surgery on both of his eyes for cataracts when he was a child. When he drew he brought his body very close to the paper.

Dance: Joy in Motion

"Mommy, dance....please."
❖ Sean, ten-year-old boy with autism

Sophie and many of the other neurodiverse youngsters I see love to dance. Movement helps to integrate the structural, emotional, and neurological shifts that occur as neurodiverse children go through their demanding lives and therapies.

Dance and movement also become ways to observe changes in gait and balance. When I dance with my young clients before and after applied touch therapy sessions, we always smile. Those smiles brighten even the most wintry days. They stay with you like eternal lights.

Parents and therapists can learn to mirror a child's movement for integrative purposes. I do this often with my clients. All of these kinds of movement interventions differ from using dance and movement as psychotherapy. The movement I do is generally for the purposes of structural integration. You can also explore dance more specifically as a form of psychological or somatic therapy.

Figure 7.2 Mirroring and Elongating

The American Dance Therapy Association conducts research and supports investigations using their interventions. In fact, Dance Therapy was born out of an experimental use of movement for adults who were mentally challenged.

From the perspective of the American Dance Therapy Association "dance/movement therapy is the psychotherapeutic use of movement which furthers the emotional, cognitive, physical and social integration of the individual." (American Dance Therapy Association 2009) There are certified dance/movement therapists who are trained to help children with special needs to deepen body awareness and recognition of self and others in dynamic movement. Proprioception and hyper- and hypo-sensitivity can be balanced in movement experiences tailored to individual children. Parents can also learn from trained therapists how to follow through with movement explorations at home.

The American Dance Therapy Association (ADTA) can put you in touch with certified therapists in the US. In the UK the Association for Dance Movement Psychotherapy UK (ADMPUK) serves the same purpose and in Australia there is the International Dance Therapy Institute of Australia (IDTIA).

Equine Therapy: Limbic Stimulation through Contact with Horses

"I am absolutely nuts about horses." (Grandin)
❖ Temple Grandin (in an interview)

Equine therapy has played a significant role in Sophie's life and has promoted her structural health since she was small. It has also gifted her with lasting relationships including with the horses she has ridden. Horses react to the emotions and energy of their surroundings. They are the embodiment of simple and bonding mammalian intelligence. Therapeutic riding is an experience of trust and rhythmic entrainment. Riding forces the rider to engage core muscles and merge that experience with the horse's gait. This creates a felt sense of supported, interactive relationship. Balance, muscular tone, motor development and structural alignment evolve from this relationship. I remember watching wide-eyed as

Sophie's scoliosis virtually disappeared when she rode her horse with the support of her Occupational Therapist.

NARHA, now called PATH (Professional Association of Therapeutic Horsemanship), has a database of accredited equine therapy centers. They are a resource for research, training and detailed descriptions of the benefits of therapeutic riding. This is an international organization.

The Horse Boy Foundation was founded by Rupert Isaacson and his wife Kristin following their profound experience of the way in which horse riding and related experiences transformed their autistic son Rowan. They created a system that uses horse riding as an approach to developing language, communication and social engagement for neuro-psychiatric conditions. Many parents of autistic children come to realize that they do not need to find a cure or try to fix their children. Like Elaine Hall who I refer to in the section on Theater and Film, Rupert and Kristin seek to innovate ways to enhance their son's wholeness and brilliance and to extend what they learn to others. They see, as does Jonathan Mooney who is discussed in the section on Learning Challenges, that there is nothing wrong with the child and that the work is in educating others about neurodiversity.

Music: Using Sound, Rhythm, Listening and Hearing for Sensory Integration

"Music is a swift weaver of deep feelings." (Campbell 2009, p.37)

❖ Andres Segovia

Every one of Sophie's therapy sessions includes music. In his book *The Mozart Effect for Children* musicologist Don Campbell says,

> You don't need a perfect understanding of the brain to use music to encourage health in development. All you need to do is play a wide variety of recorded music, actively make music with your child in as many fun ways as you can, and open your child's ears to all the ways in which music can help him be smarter and more aware and in control of his emotions. (Campbell 2009, first published 2000, p. 32)

Campbell's book is replete with suggestions on how to playfully invite music into the lifestyle of a neurodiverse child. His suggestions for the use of music in niche construction can be translated directly to the use of art, dance and story making.

The American Music Therapy Association promotes and publishes research using music as therapy for children with autism. Two recent studies include investigating whether music promotes the capacity to pay attention in relationship and whether autistic children can identify emotion in music. Both of these studies are posted on the American Music Therapy Association website.

Music is a non-threatening form of non-verbal communication. It has its own structure and is a language that can speak to some neurodiverse children and youth. It is one of Howard Gardner's identified intelligences. (Gardner 1983) Music charges the limbic brain, stimulating the creative and motivational circuits. Listening to music and actively engaging in music making, as Don Campbell suggests, can entrain the brain to organized rhythms and reduce stress. Engaging with sound can potentially arouse neuronal growth. (Gardner 1983)

Music for Autism is a nonprofit organization based in the UK but now offering programs in the US as well. It was started by parents of an autistic child who believed that music creates bonding. The organization sponsors cost free autism friendly interactive concerts in environments that support neurodiversity. Award winning musicians like Sir James Galway offer not only their great music but also their engaged presence to transmit the power of music to awaken innate intelligence.

Nordoff-Robbins Music Therapy, Auditory Integration Training, Rhythmic Entrainment Integration and the Tomatis Listening Centers are just some of the international organizations that present different systems for using sound, rhythm and tone to enhance the innate capacities of the brain to be resilient.

Nature Based Therapies: Allowing the Natural World to be an Ally

"When visitors called I hid in the hayloft and lay hidden behind the great heap of hay while a servant was calling my name in the yard." (Yeats 2010 p.49)
  ❖ William Butler Yeats

My studio in Colorado is in a pristine environment, surrounded by nature. Sophie loves to come there where every window looks out at a mountain range or a broad field. Cathy, her mother, has always made it a point to bring nature to Sophie and to bring Sophie to nature. Whether in the touch of the seeds she puts in her daughter's hand or the bark of a tree that she invites her to stroke, Cathy invests in Sophie's experience of nature. The natural world is a model of sensory integration. Nature is a sanctuary as it was for Yeats as a child who feared the judgment of people because of his awkwardness and speech difficulties. (Yeats 2010) Notice how a child changes in relationship to the elements of nature. What is her response to water, to trees, to wind, to flowers, mountains, shade and sun? Nature is a mirror. Wherever you are, even in the most urban environment, you can find nature. In fact, we are nature. It is always with us. I remember as a child in the Bronx, New York spending hours immersed in reflections on the sky, especially at night. This eased my troubled mind and calmed my agitated body. The heavens were spacious and unconditional enough to invite my imagination and my imagination soothed my nervous system.

A child may show a preference or attraction to a particular element in nature. Use aquatic therapy, for instance, for a child who is drawn to water (see Swimming/Aquatic Therapy) or who is calmed by water. If a child is obsessively in motion, consider neurodevelopmental movement therapies. The element of fire is frequently associated with creativity. A child with a fiery personality may be asking for more art in his life. The TARA Approach offers an abundance of resources on the relationship between the elements in nature and behavior and health. The rhythms of nature evoke an entrainment that stabilizes neurology. The story in Chapter Six that Aila wrote is a compelling example of how nature becomes a refuge for a struggling child.

Outdoor education and wilderness experiences for neurodiverse children are more often geared towards adolescents than youngsters. They also frequently have a summer camp type of design. Obviously it is critical to review the ethical and safety standards of these programs and make a thorough on-site assessment of their accommodations. Some outdoor experiences provide one-on-one aides and communication technology to foster social engagement as well as nature immersion. As Sophie has matured she has attended these camps independently and developed lasting relationships with other campers and aides. Staff should be well trained in services to neurodiverse children with expertise in adjunctive communication devices and multiple intelligences. This is a field ripe for exploration, development and research.

The applied touch system that I teach and use in my clinical trials is a nature based system. It reminds children that they are part of nature. "We all have a birthright to be part of the vitality that is unceasing in the natural world. The five primary elements of the natural world are within us. Contacting them is a sure route to ending separation." (Mines 2003, p.196) When I teach children how to balance the elements within them with the simple playful practice of holding their fingers (Mines 1998, pp.2-5) I am guiding them back into nature. I usually give them finger puppets that are color coded to the elements to help them remember the correlations between each finger and each element. Every child, without exception, who has learned this simple practice loves it and their parents report back to me in a manner similar to this message I received from the mother of an autistic child who was very withdrawn and secretive: "Lydia has become much more aware of her feelings since you taught her about the elements and her fingers and she tells her friends about them too. They gather around her, pay close attention and imitate her finger holds. This makes her very happy."

Poetry, Story-Making and Storytelling: Creative Avenues for Language Development and Communication

"I can kiss you quietly with gorgeous marvelous thoughts." (Ball 1998)
❖ Marshall Ball

Sophie, Aila, and Aubrey and I used storytelling and story making long before they used computer technology. When they began to use devices we translated that practice for those applications. Children and youth with sensory challenges deepen their experiences and relationships to language when they make their own stories. The articulation of their inner words is a relief to their nervous systems and enhances their language skills. I encourage language development and communication as a potent avenue for neuronal development including for those who are non-verbal. Young people who do not use words nevertheless respond to and comprehend them. Computer technology and language augmentation devices can become extensions of their inner voices.

Neurodiverse children need direction to deepen their relationship with language and to articulate their inner worlds in ways that are satisfying. The cues about storytelling and story-making in Chapter Six of this book bring into your homes and your therapy rooms the liberating worlds of stories and writing. I have always stood up for language development and communication as potent avenues for nervous system balance and neuronal development, including, and perhaps especially for those who are non-verbal.

Carly Fleishman is referred to frequently in this book. She began to write by just leaning over to type on an available nearby lap top. Now she tells other autistic children to "never give up because your inner voice will find its way out." (Fleischmann, C. 2012) Carly writes about how her brain works and is finishing a novel that includes her vision for humanity. You can see YouTube videos about Carly, read her blog and receive her Tweets. As an adolescent with a rich interior life, Sophie is also developing a blog and I am her cheerleader.

Marshall Ball is an autistic man who does not speak or walk. He began to write poetry by pointing to picture symbols in a children's book with his forehead while he was sitting in his mother's lap. She recognized that he was trying to communicate and eventually built an alphabet board for him to spell out his poems. No technology here! Now as an adult he has a blog and his poetry is performed in multimedia productions. His poems are collected in *The Kiss of God: the Wisdom of the Silent Child*. (Ball 1999)

Marshall's parents read to him and shared their lives with him in intelligent, enriching conversation from the earliest moment possible. They never interacted with him as if he was deficient. In this way, led by faith and without external therapeutic direction or technology, they constructed a niche environment in order to unleash the wise, loving and metaphoric language of their son. The internet and self-publishing are outlets Marshall's parents use to share his writing with the world. Many other neurodiverse authors use these avenues. They are a cadre of courageous artists tearing down the walls of intolerance, ignorance and false, misleading assumptions about their intelligence.

Swimming/Aquatic Therapy: The Benefits of Movement in Water for Sensory Integration

"Swimming has an advantage over team sports for autistic children because the focus is on the individual." (Landa 2012)
❖ Rebecca Landa, Director, Center for Autism and Related Disorders/Kennedy Krieger

Sophie has been swimming most of her life. Being in the water is a sensory rich experience. When a group of Occupational Therapists who use aquatic therapy were asked about the young children with autism who they were treating in the water, a majority of them noticed significant shifts after treatment in eye contact, tolerating touch, attention, proprioception and balance. (Vonder Hulls, Walker, and Powell 2006, pp. 13-22) Bobbing up and down or moving on all planes in the water affects the body in the same way as jumping on a trampoline, providing vestibular input.

Aquatic training is a safety measure for autistic children who, like all children, are vulnerable to danger in the water when they are without skills. One exceptionally hot summer I was working with a family with an autistic nine year old daughter. During our breaks her mother took her for a swim at our local fresh water pool. She returned to our sessions by bursting into the room and striking a victorious pose, completely awakened from her typically withdrawn state. This was a visible testimony to the power of swimming for an autistic child.

Michael Phelps, record setting Olympic gold medalist, started swimming to cope with ADHD. Swimming helped him focus his energy and excel. He has become a role model for many aspiring sensory challenged athletes.

The Aquatic Therapy and Rehab Institute, the National Drowning Prevention Alliance and USA Swimming all conduct training programs, do clinical research and provide opportunities for neurodiverse and differently-abled children and their families to gain confidence and skill in the water. Swimming can be learned in a functional context that enhances motor coordination, strength and endurance. Children with difficulties on land frequently find themselves free of those difficulties in the water. Sensory and motor deficits do not inhibit skill in the water when mentorship and attuned instruction is available. Most importantly when safety and support are provided, swimming is exhilarating fun.

Theater and Film: Living Literature

"I am no longer concerned about what is 'normal.' Though I once yearned to fit in like everyone else, I have come to realize that the 'normal' I was seeking was actually a search for self-acceptance. Through the rigors of life and the grace of God, I have found that acceptance and taken from it a sense of peace. Beyond that the 'normal' I so desperately craved has been trumped by the miraculous." (Hall 2010, p. 273)

❖ Elaine Hall, founder of The Miracle Project, a theater and film program for children of all abilities and the HBO Emmy Award winning documentary *Autism: The Musical*

A recent study by members of ASHA (American Speech-Language-Hearing Association) has shown that high school students with autism who participated in theater classes demonstrated an increase in social interaction and language skills. A theater environment is also a social environment. Neurodiverse students involved in rehearsal and performances of a show became more sensitive to others' feelings and were more likely to offer help to others when needed. (American Speech-Language-Hearing Association 2011)

Elaine Hall who is an acting coach and the mother of an autistic son created the ground-breaking Miracle Project. The evolution of that program is portrayed in her book *Now I See the Moon* that chronicles the life changing passage that began the moment she adopted her son from an orphanage in Russia.

Video is an easy and accessible way to spread ideas. Videos can also be used as journals, documentation of growth and development, and as a way to track the progress of therapeutic interventions. The treasury of films on YouTube can be surveyed by parents and clinicians to select appropriate videos to view as mentorship. It is inspiring to see how many neurodiverse individuals have generously opened their hearts on video so that the assumptions we have erroneously made about being neurodiverse can be dispelled. This has led to the emergence of a vital, innovative art form and outlet that is relatively easy to use and accessible to many.

I encourage Sophie, Aubrey and Alia in directions that will convey to a broad audience what they have learned about expression, including through videos. All media are fair game for neurodiverse people who want to speak to the world that needs to hear them. This is the very essence of what niche construction means.

Enhancement Resources and Niche Construction

Neurodiverse children and youth almost always respond well to supportive modalities like Occupational, Physical and Speech therapies, augmentative devices, products and tools that are like yoga props for the skills they cannot easily access. These resources extend to them a felt sense of capacities that once seemed remote like verbal communication, upright alignment, movement flexibility, expression of feelings, and containment alongside interaction with others, hearing, speaking, focusing and learning. Some devices are very expensive but can be replicated by resourceful, creative parents as Marshall Ball's mother describes in her introductions to her son's books and on his website. As you create niche constructions for neurodiverse children consider these options.

Applications for Computers and Hand-Held Devices: Finding Your Voice

"Walking with a friend in the dark is better than walking alone in the light." (Keller 2005)
❖ Helen Keller

New apps (computer applications) for neurodiverse children, youth and adults are developing rapidly to make learning and communication possible where it was not before. Sometimes you can find these for free for autistic children or children with learning challenges. It just takes some diligent investigation. Sophie's eye gaze device, for instance, helps her to focus. This then functions as a sensory filter as well as a communication medium.

It is worth noting that the most successful apps were and are being developed by people who are themselves neurodiverse. Steve Jobs perhaps unwittingly created tools that are neurodiverse and sensory friendly. His emphasis on design simplicity and the structures and systems that shape his iPad in particular have been turned into learning tools for autistic students. It is very likely that it was his own neurodiversity that oriented him in this direction (Isaacson and Baker 2011).

Bill Gates and Krista Caudill, on the other hand, deliberately created apps for differently abled people. Microsoft, in partnership with Intergen, has designed easily accessible apps for anyone who has Microsoft Word that brings the world of the internet to the blind and the deaf. (ONE News 2011). You can view a video of Neal Jarvis of the Royal New Zealand Foundation for the Blind talking about the Microsoft apps.

Krista Caudill of the University of Delaware who is deaf and blind developed systems that have both learning and interactive aspects to make it possible for blind and deaf students to become participatory learners in the classroom. (ONE News 2011)

There is no doubt that apps will continue to evolve at a rapid pace and make ongoing contributions to lessen the sense of isolation in the neurodiverse world. I do want to emphasize that apps can never replace human contact but when you combine the two the result is magical.

Applied Touch: Sensory Integration is in Your Own Hands

"Skin cannot shut its eyes or cover its ears. It is in a constant state of readiness to receive messages." (Field 2003, p. 77)
❖ Tiffany Field, Director of the Touch Research Institute at the University of Miami School of Medicine

Applied touch is a genre that encompasses all the hands-on, non-invasive interventions. It has been a part of Sophie's sensory integration for over six years. It is woven into her daily life. Her mother brings applied touch with her wherever she goes and offers it to Sophie whenever she needs it. Hospital visits, social encounters, shopping trips, family gatherings all have the potential to be overwhelming to Sophie's sensory system but the handy (pun intended) use of applied touch changes overwhelm to calm every time. Educated touch balances bioelectrical frequencies to create a state of ease. Western medicine already uses the body's bioelectrical field for diagnostic testing with imaging technology. Eastern medicine has, for thousands of years, identified bioelectrical sites for treatment to align the mind and the body, but this paradigm is much newer in the West.

The 1970's and 80's were political, cultural and scientific watersheds. Healthcare was impacted by a spike in the interest in Eastern medicine. With a particular emphasis on acupuncture, Eastern modalities were introduced in a variety of settings to support everything from relaxation to pain relief. Fusions of Eastern and Western approaches to wellbeing evolved. The general public was magnetized to these innovative concepts when allopathic approaches failed to relieve afflictions like depression, trauma, inflammation and relentless pain.

From the wellsprings of this infusion came systems that used acupuncture and related systems. Others were entirely Western in orientation like Cranial-Sacral therapies and Applied Kinesiology (muscle testing). Many of these forms of applied touch were grouped as sub-categories of massage and were often incorporated into massage treatments. One cornerstone of applied touch introduced in this book is that it calms the primitive and limbic brain structures to free up higher functions. Some applied touch, like massage, can be vigorous and manipulates tissue, but the protocols here do not require anything like that. Touch is adjusted to the recipient's tolerance. This distinguishes Jin Shin TARA from virtually all other applied touch therapies.

Research is accelerating as scientists and therapists become more interested in applied touch systems. I used the applied touch methodology in this book for young children diagnosed with autism and intend to continue with other research along these lines. (Mines, Morris and Persun, 2012, in press, *inter alia*) Several trials have been done with acupuncture especially since the National Institute of Health acknowledged its efficacy for chronic pain, inflammatory and gynecological disorders in 2007. There are overviews summarizing the studies done throughout the world using acupuncture for the treatment of autism. Some are listed in our bibliography. (Young 2010)

The Touch Research Institute at the University of Miami's School of Medicine conducts ongoing research into the role of subtle touch on babies and children who have neurodevelopmental struggles. (Finando 2008) Dr. Stephen Porges made a huge contribution to the field of applied touch when he began to do research on the Social Engagement System and its relationship to autism. (Porges 2004) His development of the Polyvagal Theory continues to generate research and experimentation with how touch can gently liberate the cranial nerves. A variety of applied touch practitioners with both Eastern and Western orientations have rallied to Dr. Porges' Polyvagal Theory, developing different approaches, particularly after the promising results of his research at the Listening Project at the University of Chicago.

Given that the concept of applied touch for neurobiological imbalances is quite new in the West, it is only natural to view research as evolving. The TARA Approach will continue to conduct research projects to demonstrate the value of applied touch, particularly when treatment is replicated at home by the children themselves and parents.

My article on titrating touch for children with special needs (Mines 2010, pp. 34-43) is an essential pacing guide alongside the principle offered throughout this book of following the child. With these caveats in mind there is absolutely no reason not to include applied touch in your niche construction.

Augmented Communication: Supporting Articulation for People Who Are Sensory Challenged and Non-verbal

"I thought I would have to teach my daughter about the world. It turns out I have to teach the world about my daughter. They see a girl who cannot talk. I see a miracle that doesn't need words."
❖ Mother of a Girl with Rett Syndrome

This mother is right. Non-verbal children need to communicate so that the world can understand them in their language. This is what Sophie is doing when she writes her stories, makes her sounds, paints, dances, and speaks through her eye gaze device. Augmentation that makes it possible for non-verbal children to be heard is a technological blessing.

Augmentation that allows communication through typing, language boards or even a simple home-made alphabet board such as Marshall Ball's mother made for him, create community.

Simple Velcro switches on a board give non-verbal children a choice. (The Center for AAC & Autism 2009) Sophie used these for years. The International Rett Syndrome Foundation Communication and Device Information Exchange is a place where parents, teachers, therapists and anyone working with communication devices can share ideas, ask questions or start a dialogue. Eye gaze and eye typing devices are undergoing continuous development. They, like PECS (picture exchange cards) only work when advocating, highly interactive adults prepare programs and organize information on the device. This should be underscored. These devices require a high level of parent and caregiver involvement. Aides, teachers and anyone involved in the user's world needs careful mentoring in the programing of the device and its use as a medium of expression, communication and social engagement.

Devices that augment communication are only useful when they are thoroughly integrated into the learning environment and individually programmed. All the information in the device has to be tailored so that the device becomes an intimate, individuated expression of the child's world. It is almost like the device represents the child's private diary or journal, sharing with the world the people and the experiences that matter to them. The principles of attunement, theory of mind and brain to brain communication are essential in the creation of a truly representative augmented communication device. Some speech therapists are trying to create an augmented communication device that actually reproduces the child's voice as it is heard when they are sounding.

Learning Challenges: Multiple Intelligences and the Right to Successful Learning

"The definition of a learning disability is not a defective brain. It is a different brain in a defective system." (Mooney 2011)
❖ Jonathan Mooney

In the exploration of niche construction to optimize limbic stimulation for autistic young people and those with sensory challenges we have to look at the learning environment and its role in sensory integration. Neurodiverse children usually struggle to learn in a typical classroom that requires them to sit still at a desk and learn on only two planes: the linguistic and the logical. We now know that there is nothing wrong with children who can't learn this way though but historically we made them wrong and labeled them "learning disabled." Beginning in 1983 when Howard Gardner published his theory of multiple intelligences we have had the option to correct our course. Nevertheless it is sadly still necessary for parents to make a stand for special needs children in many classrooms. This is true for Cathy, Sophie's mom, just as it was true for Loretta, Aubrey's mom, and for many other parents of neurodiverse youth. If Cathy did not visit Sophie's classroom frequently, engage with teachers and aides, participate and encourage attentiveness and engagement, Sophie would likely be more passive and sometimes overlooked in school.

Some schools are pressured to pigeon hole a child's experience. As the mother of a child who fell through the cracks in testing and who school officials tried to categorize I know whereof I speak. Like educational activist Jonathan Mooney who was told he would end up "flipping burgers or in prison", I was outraged when I was told that my daughter would "do better in a technical program." She is now, as I write this, in a graduate degree program at an excellent university.

Jonathan Mooney, author of *The Short Bus* (Mooney 2007) and founder of Project Eye to Eye, a revolutionary mentorship model of learning, has taken Howard Gardner's theories of multiple intelligences to the streets. Mooney believes that the onus of responsibility is on the educators to change how we direct children whose brains are wired differently. Gardner articulated at least eight ways of learning and leaves the door open for more. The movement out of the deficit learning disability paradigm into the celebration of neurodiversity is the corrective direction we must take. Familiarizing yourself with the concepts of multiple intelligences is an important step in reframing how you view learning in general and neurodiversity in particular. It will also help to build niche construction at home and in the schools. When these environments are reflective of each other in this regard the neurodiverse child is consistently encouraged to maximize potential.

Thom Hartmann, like Jonathan Mooney, sees the increase in learning challenges as a compass for the future. (Hartmann and Palladino 2005) If you are the parent or therapist of a child who has been labeled with "learning disabilities" I recommend that you question the structure that is doing the labeling and seek supportive guidance that evolves from your own careful and compassionate assessment of your child or your patient. Karen Lowry's saga of her long journey to the essence of her son through the labyrinthine world of school diagnostics is worth reading. (Lowry 2008). It is a cautionary tale. It leads to the homeland of advocacy and teaching self-advocacy as the primary antidote to "learning disabilities" or "learning challenges." The question is who is really challenged? Is it the child or is it the educational systems?

"If your child is diagnosed with any kind of learning disability, have his hearing tested before accepting the diagnosis as complete," says music educator and author Don Campbell. The same can be said for vision testing. Children may well be struggling in school because they need to learn actively, through their bodies, and the school environment may restrict them from doing that. (Campbell 2009) Read Chapter One in this book for an overview of the relationship between the sensory systems and learning.

I strongly recommend that you watch the YouTube video of Jonathan Mooney's presentation at the Inclusive Education Conference in Denver, Colorado in 2011. (Mooney 2011) Other resources in this compilation and throughout this book can lead you to learning supports that enhance a child's life without inferring that they are deficient. Children never are deficient. My experience is that children want to learn and always will when they are welcomed into learning and when their sensory, mechanical and structural needs are met. Children lead us to find new ways of learning. Indeed they are constantly learning wherever they are. Let's follow where they lead. This is what Sophie, Aubrey and Alia, and all my young friends have taught me.

Neurodevelopmental Occupational Therapy

"The brain becomes what it does." (Perry and Szalavitz 2011, p.230)
❖ Bruce Perry

The simple, natural tasks of living, learning, relating and growing that are not so simple for children with sensory inefficiencies are the domain of Occupational Therapy (OT). A neurodevelopmental approach enhances how OT is used for autism and sensory integration. Speech and Physical therapists, as well as any other healthcare professionals can be trained to take a neurodevelopmental approach. Limbic stimulation is heightened when functional body mechanics are aligned and balanced. Neurodiversity is often accompanied by structural issues that perpetuate compensatory patterns. All children, regardless of their sensory needs, including those with spasticity and severe restrictions, can be assisted mechanically to find their functional capacities, structural integrity and optimum physiological potential through OT and other therapies. (Landrigan, Lambertini and Birnbaum 2012)

Physical Therapy: The Value of Sequenced Manual Therapy for Sensory Integration

"Renewed interest is being focused on the critical interaction between motor patterning (coordinated use of the body) and the development of cognitive skills." (Healy 2004, first published 1987, p.164)
❖ Jane M. Healy, Ph.D.

Sequenced Physical Therapy (PT) goes to the heart of the integration of the primary sensory systems and the external senses. "Speaking in general terms, with cranial nerve entrapment the ability to discern sensory input can be stressed causing the child to be hypersensitive (over-sensitive) or hyposensitive (withdrawn), or a mixture of the two. During birth cranial entrapment can occur due to the compressive forces on the cranium. In a Caesarean delivery cranial nerve entrapment can also occur due to the positioning of the head." (Jones 2012)

Sequenced manual therapy blends beautifully with all other therapies, including OT. Recent research (Mines, Morris and Persun 2012, (in press, *inter alia*) shows that the combination of applied touch, physical therapy and occupational therapy is more effective in stimulating social engagement and learning then physical or occupational therapy alone. Sophie and all the others you meet in these pages are models of my research results. They all receive ongoing Speech, Physical and Occupational Therapy, but it was when we began to include applied touch and other aspects of the TARA Approach like limbic stimulation, integrating the arts into niche construction and finding and attuned family centered orientation, that her social engagement and learning accelerated.

Relaxation-Visualization: Inner Focus for Sensory Integration

"Create a quiet place in your home and always go there when rest and relaxation are needed. It can be a place in a room, a place outside, or even just a chair or a couch. Get into the habit of always going to the same place. The repetition itself is relaxing." (Finando 2008, p. 160)
❖ Donna Finando, L.Ac, LMT

Sophie's mom finds and creates relaxing music and soothing environments for her daughter knowing how hard Sophie works all the time in order to function. Cathy takes Sophie's relaxation music with her wherever she goes, providing a portable niche construction. Relaxing interludes and visualizations send organizing messages to the nervous system. Parents can create relaxation and visualization audios and program them onto whatever device is available. Select music based on the individual child's responses rather than assumptions. Visualizations and music can be combined with applied touch. Identifying a safe place and going there visually is a time tested successful visualization. Waterfall music combined with a visualization of water imagery can soften hypertensive habituation. You can focus on the senses that need particular support. If your child has difficulty feeling a relationship to gravity, for instance, you can create visualizations that depict being supported by the earth. An example would be inviting a child to imagine that the earth was holding them up by feeling their contact with the ground, the floor or whatever surface they were resting on, more and more. Breath can be used to enhance the experience of sinking down onto the earth. The #6 area, on the sole side of the foot (see Figure 5.1), is an area that stimulates an experience of being grounded and rooted and could be held on both the right and left sides simultaneously during such a visualization. Your theory of mind and attunement to the child builds the visualization and individualizes it for them.

Some children relax when they are compressed. For information about this see the section that follows on Structural Supports. One autistic child I know uses a big spandex sack that she climbs inside when she needs space to integrate and calm down. She feels more spacious when she is compressed. After watching her daughter use it for years her mom decided to try it too! It worked for her as well!

Other children may relax more deeply if they have space to themselves. A young boy with Tourette's syndrome was completely relieved of his chronic tics through a combination of applied touch self-care and going inside a tent that he erected with his parents with the understanding that he could go inside it whenever he felt stressed. A similar approach was effective for a ten year old girl diagnosed with hyperactivity and Reactive Attachment Disorder. When her parents allowed her to create a space in her home that was entirely and solely her own and to go there whenever she felt the need, her symptoms diminished considerably. Punishments and consequences became largely irrelevant when she had the space she need for herself.

In the Chapter Five on applied touch there are simple treatments that calm the nervous system and produce rest and relaxation. When these are matched with visualizations. The benefits of both are increased. For instance, you can ask a child to hold their fingers, one at a time, as you lead them through a safe place visualization. Done with relaxing music in the background this is a formula for unwinding. I used it recently in the car when my grandchildren were dangerously rambunctious and it worked like a charm. If the combination of visualization, applied touch and music is over-stimulating, simply subtract one component.

You can make a relaxation kit of music, applied touch recipes, and visualization scenarios and take it with you wherever you go so that it is at the ready at family events, appointments, medical procedures, outings, and even in restaurants.

Relaxation integrates the mind and the body. Be creative and test your relaxation trial runs on yourself. When the adults who serve neurodiverse children are relaxed it communicates even without words or interventions to the child. Your relaxation may be central to a child's ability to relax.

Speech Therapy: Supporting Articulation and Clear Communication for Sensory Integration

"We owe a debt of gratitude to our speech therapist. She not only was instrumental in my son saying his first words. She also trained us so that we could help him at home. After all, we are with him all the time."

❖ Mother of a boy with autism who began speech therapy at two years

Even though Sophie is largely non-verbal she has received weekly speech therapy for most of her life. This has made a great contribution to her interactive and feeling vocabulary. Though she does not say many words she knows their meanings and implements emotional language in her expressions and gestures. She moves towards people with expressive feeling and responds to their feelings appropriately such as comforting people who are sad or laughing at jokes. She tests all her communication devices in speech therapy sessions to gain accuracy and proficiency as well as programming her emotional language and basic needs. Speech therapy for a neurodiverse child is not just about saying words correctly. It is about language, communication, social engagement, word concepts, and theory of mind, empathy, reading facial expressions, voice tone and body language. It is as much about non-verbal communication as it is about verbalizing. Speech therapists also help non-verbal children with augmentation devices. Sophie's Speech Therapist understands the meaning content of Sophie's sounding and responds appropriately. She engages with Sophie in deeply curious ways to inquire into the feeling content of Sophie's internal experience. She uses art and articulation, alongside augmentation devices, to have meaningful conversations with Sophie and to build their authentic relationship.

Speech Therapists also attend to the development of the muscles related to speech. They may use manual therapies for the face and the mouth to support speech. Evaluating the muscle tone of a child's mouth is a delicate and important aspect of a Speech Therapist's role requiring acute sensitivity to the child. All the parameters about pacing and following the child that are discussed throughout this book are applicable in this environment.

Children with auditory issues also have speech-language difficulties and may appear to be unable to find the right word or engage in conversation. They will benefit from seeing an attuned SLP or Speech-Language Pathologist. Aubrey, who I told you about in the previous chapter, worked with a SLP and combined that therapy with applied touch to minimize his shuttering so that he could participate more comfortably in learning and social environments with his peers. Only under extreme stress does his stutter return and now, as a young adult, he knows that this is the signal to back off and take care of himself.

The American Speech-Language-Hearing Association (ASHA) provides information about Speech Therapy and certified therapists. Apraxia Speaks is an organization that collects information and resources about that particular disorder.

Structural Supports: Using Compression for Sensory Integration

(Including compressive and weighted devices)

"Everyone should have at least sixteen hugs a day." (Gerber 2012)

❖ Trigg Gerber, LMT and Mother of Three Neurodiverse Children

For some neurodiverse children compression creates relaxation. Compression clothing can be found in the athletic section of any store and can be relatively inexpensive. It is also easy to find websites that sell weighted blankets, vests and similar garments. Weighted belts and other devices can stimulate proprioception. (Sensory Processing Disorder 2012). Be sure to be careful about the weights of these items relative to the weight of the child and the recommended duration for the use of them. Consultation with an Occupational and/or Physical Therapist with training in sensory integration is helpful in choosing which devices to use. Remember that these devices can be dangerous so educate yourself about their use.

An easy way to make a weighted blanket is to insert beanbags into each quilt patch of a comforter. Never leave a small child unattended with a weighted blanket and never cover his face with the blanket. Lindsey Biel and Nancy Peske provide important guidelines for weighted and pressure materials in their book *Raising a Sensory Smart Child.* (Biel and Peske 2009, pp. 113-116)

A body sock is a Lycra-type cocoon that zips up and allows the child to go inside when they need to feel contained. It is portable, inexpensive, comes in different colors, and can be made at home. Adults are welcome to create them to size and use them for themselves. They are remarkably effective for stress.

Temple Grandin speaks of her discovery of the "squeeze machine" for herself and how she translated it from a device that helped cattle to a device that she could use and that could then be improved upon further for others with sensory needs. This is described in her book *Thinking in Pictures* (Grandin 2006, first published 1995, p.62) and it is also portrayed in the film about her life.

Temple made a "squeeze machine" or compressive device herself so it was designed and tested to suit her. This then is the formula for using these devices. They are not quick fixes. They are demonstrations of meeting a child's sensory needs according to their individual requirements.

Vision Therapy: Seeing Clearly for Sensory Integration

"The human visual system is one of the most complex, subtle and sophisticated engineering feats that has been produced in the biological world." (Arts Dyslexia Trust 2011)

❖ Arts Dyslexia Trust, UK

The relationship between vision and sensory processing is intricate. Vision, like hearing, develops in response to many factors including emotional conditions. As a young child I struggled painfully with severe vision problems from birth. I found enormous freedom when I began vision therapy at twelve. I became devoted to the exercises and have never worn glasses since. My youngest daughter who was diagnosed with craniosynostosis at four months had rare astigmatisms that were corrected with a combination of vision therapy and cranial treatments. My daughter and I are hardly alone in finding relief as a result of vision therapy. These quotes are from the mothers of children diagnosed with autism who brought their children to vision therapists: "School is totally different for my son since we began vision therapy. He can participate now. He could not before. It is amazing." "All my child's therapeutic experiences have transformed since we began vision therapy. He was basically non-verbal before. Now he uses speech and wants to communicate and he makes eye contact with no trouble. Before vision therapy eye contact was rare."

Meir Schneider, author of *My Life, My Vision* was legally blind from childhood. (Schneider 1998) Through vision therapy and then exercises that he developed he now has virtually perfect vision. Mother and daughter, Robin and Jillian Benoit talk about vision therapy in *Jillian's Story*.(Benoit 2010) Discouraged by some in the medical profession from exploring it Robin Benoit, Jillian's mom, has the characteristic that seems to describe most of the parents and children I talk about in this book: determination. Meir Schneider put it this way in an interview when asked how he overcame his blindness: "When you succumb to your circumstances you never discover your potential." (Schneider 2010)

There are guidelines about what to look for in seeking vision therapy. In her book *Thinking in Pictures* Temple Grandin addresses the issue for children on the autism spectrum. "If visual processing problems are suspected the child should see a developmental optometrist. This is a special eye doctor who can do therapy and exercises to help the processing problems that are inside the brain. In many of these children the eye itself is normal but faulty wiring in the brain is causing the problem." (Grandin 2006, First published 1995, p. 79) Though this book was written some time ago it continues to inspire parents who feel they are struggling alone to advocate for their neurodiverse children by providing new perspectives and resources such as this one regarding vision therapy.

Good vision therapists know the difference between sight and vision and the relationship between vision and learning. Vision, motor coordination, concentration, proprioception, cognition and perception are all one in a child's holistic experience. Children struggling to see clearly are exhausted by their efforts to discern and comprehend their world. They cannot get to the root of their over-efforting and look to us to find that causation and relieve it. Adults cannot know what a child is seeing unless they inquire into their perception. Robin Benoit was a devoted and attentive mom who could not know that her daughter had double vision when Jillian was diagnosed with a different visual issue. Only when a developmentally oriented vision therapist asked Jillian gently and with real curiosity about her perceptions did this come to light. This is more evidence for how following the child is the key. Care-providers who are rushed or not tuned in to a child will miss the most important details. A child's entire future is shaped by these circumstances.

Parents need the clarity of mind to attend carefully to the nuances of their child's behavior. It takes perseverance to research interventions and find the professionals who are the best match. I have met many adults who were deprived of being able to fully explore their own potential because their neurological difference and/or their visual and auditory processing difficulties when they were children were never detected. The stories of CeCe in Chapter Six and Alex who you will meet in the next chapter tell you more about the role of visual processing as an aspect of neurodiversity.

Sometimes life makes it easier for parents to find help by presenting options serendipitously. This is how I met the compassionate and skilled vision therapist who changed my life and my learning by directing me so that I could find the capacity to see clearly. When I was twelve and thirteen, the years I did vision therapy, I expressed myself in secret by writing poetry. This is what I wrote for her.

The Woman Who Taught Me to See

When I came to her I saw everything twice. She smelled of violets. The lights were soft for our eyes.

She told me about black cats walking plush black carpets into black rooms issuing music played by a black gloved woman seated at a black piano. She made me love the black of night wherein I now safely slept.

She stretched me from the eyes. She worked my muscles and set me in the sun to cure. She threw away my glasses. She stroked my temples. Her dresses sounded silk as she moved about me in slippers.

Leaving her was an assault of white bleached white. The city fell like rocks onto my softened face. I rode home on my bike bearing her aromas (lemon verbena and violet). I rode home through one vision at a time.

I came and went, a sad young girl. She must have sat down after I left to release my pain from her hands where she had gathered it in.

Summary: The Bountiful Cornucopia

Niche construction is orchestrated by the sensory needs child herself. The adults in her world have the enlivening task of reading her to determine the niche components. This is a playful creative process in itself. It resembles solving a mystery but instead of finding the culprit you are identifying the liberators of a child's intelligence. Niche construction enhances and flows out of the evolution of theory of mind for the child. Please use this chapter as a stimulus package. While I have filled the cornucopia as full as I could, new possibilities for inclusion are appearing continually. Neurodiverse people, their family members and care-givers are daily opening more and more avenues for learning, growth and expression for their communities. This is a high spirited tribe. You may well become a contributor yourself.

Chapter Eight
The Triumphant Children and Their Families: The Path from Diagnosis to Advocacy

"It is important to not confuse current limitations that your child has with the remarkable capacities of her brain."
❖ Anat Baniel (Baniel 2012, p. 77)

The case studies I present here come from my direct experience with the families who use the resources I provide for you in this book. I want to extend my respect and admiration to the children whose lives are depicted. They continue to inspire me. In fact, I feel as if this book is written for and with these children who are the unsung heroes and heroines of our sensory overload generation.

Please note that these studies are always presented in a family context. It is virtually impossible to provide helpful resources for a child and expect that they will have an ongoing positive influence unless the entire family is engaged. In the Family Clinics I conduct I want to know who the family members are and the roles they play. I need to know how the family as a whole functions from the child's perspective. I sometimes see not only the nuclear family but the extended family members including grandparents, cousins, aunts and uncles who are an active part of the child's life. Children with special needs benefit from a therapeutic team. It is essential that all members of this team work cooperatively together just as it is essential that all family members collaborate for the child's best interest. Overt family struggles without healthy resolution increase the burden on a child's nervous system.

Frequently in these case studies the first change that occurs within the family is when the parents acquire a theory of mind for their sensory needs child. This requires that the parents develop insight into themselves and their histories so that they have a theory of mind for themselves. I am not exaggerating when I say that having a theory of mind for a child changes everything and opens a positive and transformative relational dimension that comes close to being miraculous. It is only when parents and caregivers have a theory of mind for the child that they are able to understand sensory processing from the child's perspective.

The Triumphant Children and Their Families
Alex: Visual Processing, Adoption and Family Healing

Do you remember Sergei who I introduced to you in Chapter Two? He is the boy who transformed his own wildness by sharing the miracle of his life. Sergei was adopted at a young age from an orphanage. Several families that I serve have adopted children, some of whom were placed in institutions before their adoptive parents found them. Elsewhere in this book I have spoken about the prevalence of sensory difficulties for these children. Their sensory struggles take many forms depending on a broad spectrum of conditions including their genetic and epigenetic backgrounds, the environments in which they lived before they were adopted and the situation in the families that bring them to a new home. I am also grateful to Alex and his family for sharing their story so that we can have increased insight into the sensory and attachment needs of adopted children with this background.

Those of us who are invited to help these families are required to look at the interaction between early developmental difficulties caused by little or no bonding and sensory struggles. Andrew Solomon points to the way early trauma can evoke autism. (Solomon 2012, p. 53) Sometimes the child's biographical tapestry weaves these threads very tightly. Educational and psychological testing is helpful in separating the strands from a neurological and behavioral standpoint. Interventions developed from this testing can make a significant difference in learning and growth. As someone who has specialized in the treatment of trauma I am fascinated by how positive changes within family relationships impact sensory issues.

Alex's presenting challenge was visual processing disorders including dyslexia as well as his slow processing of information in both academic and relational contexts. It took eight year old Alex a long time to complete sentences and he seemed to be disconnected when he spoke to others, even his parents. He habitually looked down when speaking or away from the person who was speaking to him.

Alex's parents contacted me to arrange a Family Clinic at the recommendation of psychologist at Alex's school who felt that there were emotional and psychological components to Alex's delayed responses. After interviewing Alex's parents and consulting with the school psychologist, I put together a picture of Alex's family life at home and his world at school.

Alex's parents were at a crossroads. Like many parents with a special needs child who have just received a diagnosis Connie and Derek were in shock. They were overwhelmed with the financial implications and extremely busy trying to earn the money they needed. There was nothing that had prepared them for this situation.

Alex could de-stress with his dad. The two would sit side by side in front of the computer, their bodies touching, their eyes directed ahead, playing computer games. His mom, on the other hand, seemed always to be pointing him towards isolation, her index finger directing him to go to his room for yet another "time out."

Alex wanted to read but the effort was painful. His head hurt and his eyes burned when he tried to focus. He squinted. He used his hands to stretch the skin around his eyes as if somehow that would allow him to see more. He rubbed his eyes a lot and with intensity. He wanted the letters to stay put, to fall into place in the right order but he did not know how to make them do that. He battled against his mother's impatience and took shelter in his father's lenience but neither of them helped him read.

My first step was to see if Connie and Derek could become a unified team. There was a lot of arguing at home and the feeling of stress was contagious. Connie and Derek had never heard about theory of mind, attachment or brain-to-brain communication despite being intelligent, well-educated people. They felt bombarded by how financial issues had suddenly imploded on their free time. Finally, they had no guidance about how the cocktail of PTSD (Post-Traumatic Stress Disorder) that Alex carried from his institutional origins mixed with his visual processing disorder.

In Alex's interest I devoted time to educating Connie and Derek about child development. They made a commitment to each other to keep their disagreements and frustrations about parenting apart and to let Alex know that their confusion was not his fault. They could admit that they were having trouble but they had to be clear that this was not Alex's problem. This was their first step in the direction of having a theory of mind for their son. Families reel under the weight of the magnitude of life change that occurs when their child or children receive sensory diagnoses. Marriages sometimes stagger and even come unglued. I knew the frequency of this disarray and serve, to the best of my ability, as an advocate for cohesion, patience and unity.

Connie and Derek had barely reached the first step on the diagnostic ladder. They were experiencing their own form of sensory overload in trying to process information about their son's learning needs. They were also a young couple and Alex was their first and only child. They did not have extended family members who lived anywhere nearby who they could call upon for counsel. These factors are not irrelevant to the diagnostic journey and the treatment of sensory needs. Connie and Derek needed allies, education, and assistance to anchor themselves so that they could anchor Alex. I considered it time well spent to be an ally, provide education and give them the space to find their bearings. Thankfully they did too.

Feeling more educated and with a clearer orientation, we now turned our attention to the tools I could make available for Alex. Given my family prism I felt that first and foremost we needed to strengthen Alex's attachment to his parents. Securing this basic bonding would relax his mind so that he could focus. His mom's punitive practices had been utterly ineffective. I explained the neurochemistry of fear and why this activated Alex's history of institutionalized adoption and neglect. Connie could let go of her failed strategies once she saw this clearly. She was, in fact, only replicating what had not worked for her as a child growing up when her parents disciplined her. Sometimes parents do that. We repeat an ineffective strategy because we can't conceive of another one.

As Connie developed a theory of mind about her son and understood that she had to approach him as an individual separate from her with entirely different needs, she was able to build a stronger connection with Alex. This in itself functioned to create more relaxation and ease in the home.

When stress in the family environment decreased Alex was more settled and struggled less with his homework. He learned to self-treat both his eyes and his frustration by holding his middle finger which helped him much more than rubbing his eyes frantically.

Alex's parents learned how to give him regular applied touch treatments. Alex loved it when his parents treated him. He had no resistance whatsoever. In fact, he melted into the quiet time they shared. His parents gently held his forehead, palming the entire area over his eyebrows (right and left #20) while simultaneously palming the base of his cranium (right and left #4). These are called the Pillars of the Brain. They are illustrated in Figures 8.1 and 8.2. Alex's parents discovered that doing these treatments before homework made it easier for Alex to sustain attention. Sometimes, if both parents were available, one would place the palms of their hands on the calves of Alex's legs (see Figure 8.5) while the other held the points of the Pillars of the Brain. More unity at home and less tension in his head led Alex to experience a softening in his eye muscles and longer periods of focus. This led him to feel positive about himself and his capacity to learn alongside his peers. His parents re-enforced this by pointing more often to his abilities rather than to his deficits. Finding a neurodevelopmentally trained ophthalmologist who provided exercises for Alex's secondary myopia and advocating for Alex to sit in the center and closer to the blackboard in class resulted in Alex feeling like he was not trying to problem solve alone, an impossible assignment for an eight-year-old. I regularly enhanced his parents' treatment repertoire and provided ongoing opportunities for them to learn how to provide creative limbic stimulation through co-participatory play, story-making and movement. These empowering practices and their nightly ritual of treatment together lessened the magnitude of Alex's dysregulation. Life seemed less out of control and much more fun.

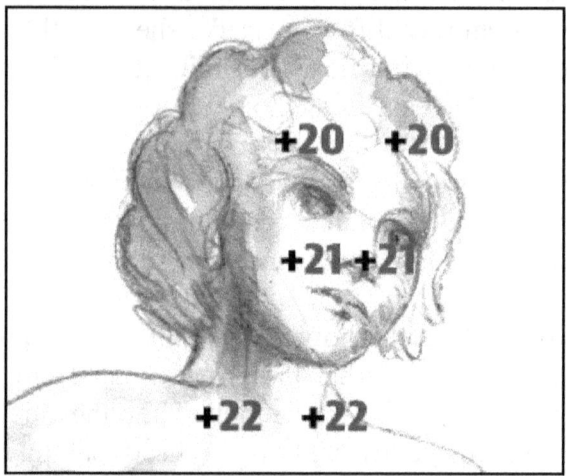

Figure 8.1 #20, #21 & #22

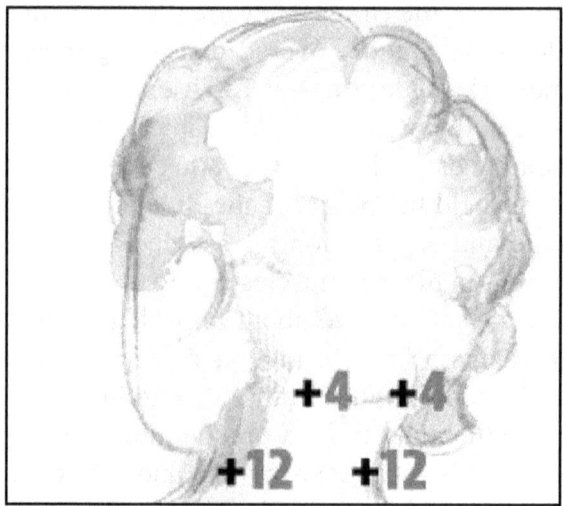

Figure 8.2 #4

The restoration of the family to their original commitment to love contributed significantly, I believe, to Alex's improved reading and learning. Alex's parents, at my recommendation, also changed some of their language when talking about him and adoption. I asked Connie to not refer to "getting Alex." Instead when she talked about his adoption she described the process as one of "finding the child she was looking for." She always made eye contact with Alex when she talked about adoption and made sure that if anyone else was there that she had his permission to speak of it. She stopped talking about how sickly, little and thin he was when she came to the orphanage. Instead she described his loving eyes and the way she felt that not only had she found him but that he had found her, and she thanked him deeply for that. She acknowledged to him that he had contributed enormously to her own growth as a person and that he had given her the gift of motherhood. You may wonder how any of this changed Alex's visual processing. Though I could speak of the role of stress in sensory processing the most succinct comment I can make is that it is much easier to see when you feel seen. I was elated when less than a year after I started seeing this family that Alex's teacher reported that he was testing at a much higher level in reading. She said his scores had "made her day."

Autism and Peer Relationships

Before I met Jonathon I met his mother, Marianne. She attended a workshop I offered for parents at an autism treatment center. A brilliant nutritionist Marianne had already explored how food and supplements could work together for higher brain functions. She had been successful in helping to calm her autistic son's sleep disturbances, but his social difficulties were still troubling. Jonathon's father was a physicist and his older sister Annette was as socially adept as Jonathon was inept. Annette readily backed off of teasing her brother for being a nerd once she was told that he was autistic. Instead she determined to reward him for how cute and smart he was and to be protective of him if others tried to ridicule him. Jonathon's preoccupation was building model structures. His father was certain he would be a structural engineer or an architect.

After recovering from the drama of testing and diagnosis, the family decided to build an excellent system of support structure for Jonathon. Marianne, in her passion for natural healing, dove into researching every intervention that had no side effects and that could be used at home. Fortunately Jonathon felt very close to his mom and was actually quite interested in her out of the box discoveries.

Jonathon got so excited about the model that he built that he would talk nonstop about them and nothing else. He was consumed by the dynamics of building but had no awareness of the architecture of relationships. He could not sense when those around him were no longer listening to his words. He did not seem to have a concept of dialogue. It was all monologues for him. Dietary change and supplements had calmed him, but he still talked at breakneck speed, without a pause and without attending to his listeners. He got so close to people when he talked to them that they became frightened but nevertheless he just kept going.

When I met Jonathon I knew that we would get along because we shared a strong, driving curiosity. In talking to him it was easy to forget that I was speaking to an eleven-year-old. It almost seemed as if Jonathon had skipped childhood entirely. He was born and then he just dove into the serious stuff.

I felt that what I could offer Jonathon was the capacity to establish and experience boundaries. Until he learned how to stop himself and make space for others he would be isolated and

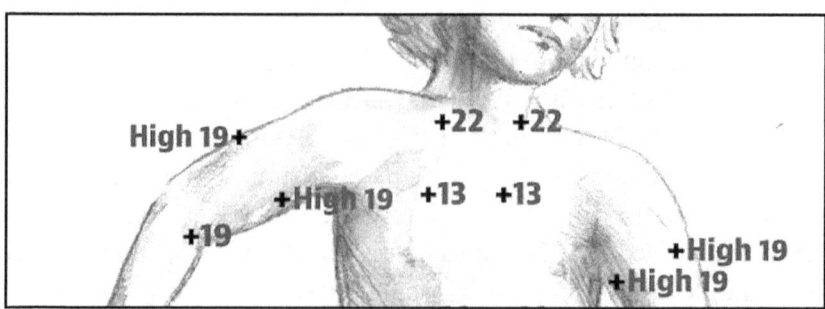

Figure 8.3 #19

dependent on his family for social engagement. Holding #19 in the bend of the elbow signals the capacity to stop, look and listen. We called it the Railroad Crossing. I modeled how Jonathon could hold #19 on both the right and left elbows simultaneously by gently placing his arms across the middle of his body so that the opposite index fingertips nestled perfectly into the bend of the elbow.

"Just obey the Railroad Crossing sign," I would remind Jonathon whenever he speeded up, became intense and verged on becoming invasive. Because holding this area produced an immediate capacity to stop, look and listen, Jonathon used it independently and eventually he was able to give himself the cues. He would fold his arms over his midline and place his fingertips in the bends of the opposite side elbows. The stance itself gave him a sense of contained safety and an awareness of his distance from others. His mother and sister practiced with him and rewarded him when they saw Jonathon giving space to others. His father eventually noticed too and applauded his son for his growth. This was the first step for Jonathon towards identifying a capacity for human dynamics. By continuing to develop nervous system containment through applied touch, Jonathon was ultimately able to cultivate reciprocal social exchanges.

Difficulty in building social relationships is a trademark of autism. I am consistently impressed and inspired by people like Jonathon who develop an enthusiastic commitment to the disciplined activities that allow them to step more fully into the world and their parents who find a way to see life through the eyes of their children.

The Value of Thorough Testing for Sensory Needs

Emma was diagnosed with autism at the age of four. She had never slept more than ninety minutes at a time. She awakened in a startle, her arms outstretched as if frantically grasping for something. She frequently regurgitated her food. Sometimes she even regurgitated water. Her behavior was confusing. She would find something infinitesimal on the floor and, no matter what it was, even a speck of dust; she appeared captivated with it, sitting in one spot, holding it, looking at it intently. When asked to relinquish it she screamed hysterically. Bright and even cherubic in appearance, with a bouncy halo of curls, she could and frequently did become clingy.

Her parents, Nadia and Otto, came to see me because of a referral from a community clinic. Together we would learn how see into the mystery of Emma's sensory needs. Because the family came to the United States from a less developed country they were unfamiliar with diagnostic defining terms and resources for sensory integration. Being multi-lingual and coming from a family that had also experienced some culture shock, I was sympathetic to their needs.

When I met Nadia and Otto I asked them, as I do with all parents, to tell me the story of Emma's early life. Emma was seated between them. I noticed that she was surprisingly non-mobile for a child of her age. She did not explore the environment as I would have expected and seemed to need the security of her parents' bodies to feel comfortable. As they spoke, however, Emma crawled in

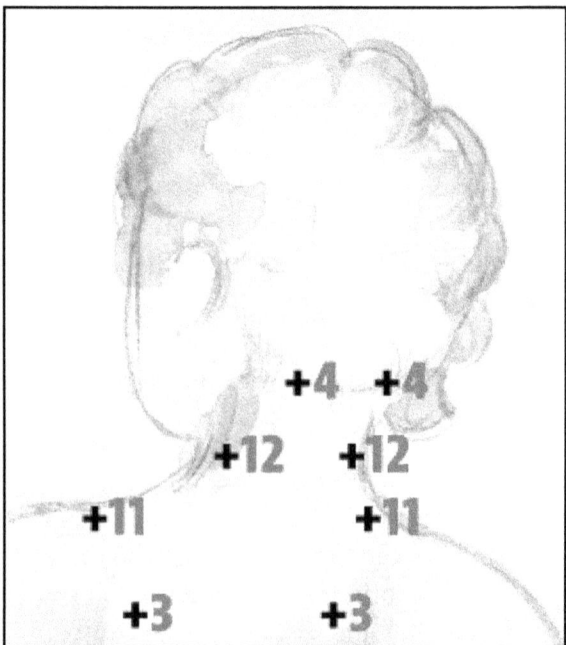

Figure 8.4 #3 and #11

my direction, more like a two-year-old than a four-year-old. Next she laid her head on my lap. Seeing the gesture as an invitation to use applied touch I asked permission of Emma and her parents to place my hands on Emma's shoulders, my fingertips contacting sites 3 and 11. I chose these sites primarily because they were so available. Sometimes that is how treatment decisions are made for children. Once you learn the map of the body you just watch to see what sites the child presents. Emma almost immediately emitted a gentle sigh of relief. In a matter of a few moments she was sound asleep in my lap.

I believe you cannot go wrong when you follow a child's lead. The applied touch that I used at Emma's invitation is a treatment I learned from my teacher, Mary Iino Burmeister, to take off what she called "the yoke of over-responsibility." As Emma slept Nadia, Otto and I talked in quiet tones about how family stressors, including the loss of an earlier pregnancy and a family history of emotional problems, were weighing on them. I suggested that the most important step to take in the moment was to not allow their daughter to carry any of the weight of their concerns and for them to feel they had the capacity to steward her. I taught them how to use this simple unburdening treatment for her as a start in their reorientation. I also taught them the wonderfully simple practice

Figure 8.5 Palming the Calves

of palming the calves that soothes the nervous system and relieves feelings of grief. This is likely my most popular intervention.

Recognizing that a child will carry unexpressed stress and that parents have to deliberately remove this from their shoulders is the form theory of mind first took for Otto and Nadia. Nadia and Otto had been told that Emma was autistic but they did not really understand what that meant. I could explain that autism changes how children develop and that the chemistry and the structure of the brain were involved. I told them that there were many kinds

Figure 8.6 11/14 Release

of autism and that no one really knows what the causes are yet but research was continuing. The family's genetic history might well be playing a role. Given that Emma also had digestive problems it seemed to me that additional testing could help clarify the situation. Applied touch would likely help alleviate her symptoms and make life somewhat easier but testing could help illuminate some of their origins.

I provided a simple treatment design of holding two areas together (#11 and #14) on the same side, treating one side and then the other, that would simultaneously calm Emma's nervous and digestive systems. Otto and Nadia treated Emma daily and noticed a decrease in her crying spells and reflux. Her elimination also improved.

Otto and Nadia consulted with the physician at the clinic that had referred them to me. Emma was tested for allergies and certain foods were eliminated from her diet. The physician also found that Emma had an inner ear infection and this was likely why she stayed so close to the ground and focused her attention there and was clingy. Otto and Nadia were relieved when these symptoms were demystified. Emma now slept through the night and was more vital. However one night she woke in a sweat with a high fever and was taken to the hospital. A sleep study was recommended and it revealed mild seizure activity. At this point I was asked to collaborate with a team of healthcare providers who could work together in Emma's best interest. The lessening of Emma's physiological burdens simplified the handling of her neurological and sensory needs and displaced other concerns. Testing that is appropriate to specific situations can uncover previously unsuspected causes of mysterious behavior.

Another child, nine-year-old Tanya, had been diagnosed with ADHD (Attention Deficit Hyperactivity Disorder). Her parents were exhausted from repeated efforts to control her out-of-bounds behaviors at home and at school, none of which were successful. Testing revealed that Tanya had a heartbeat irregularity that caused her to feel anxious and easily frustrated. This was responsible for her erratic outbursts and explosive frustrations. Teachers and family members alike had become dismayed and discouraged that they could do anything to shift Tanya's behavior. After years of extra chores, restrictions, prohibitions, medications and time-out, Tanya was finally off the hook and given the treatment she needed.

Jose and Joaquin: Expression, Creativity and Empowerment

Jose and Joaquin, brothers just two years apart, were brought to me by their mother Linda who had read my books and articles. The teachers at the school the boys attended said they were not learning at the pace that allowed them to be part of their classes. Jose, the eldest, had such severe recurrent stomach pains that he missed many days of school. Joaquin, his younger brother, could not pay attention. He moved his hands in strange ways and talked nonstop, mostly to himself, but disturbing others. He could repeat verbatim stories he heard or saw on television.

Linda would do anything for her boys and she did. After trying multiple schools in the area that turned her away she home schooled her children. While she truly loved being at home with them, Linda felt inadequate to successfully manage the way her boys behaved. Their teachers and the family pediatrician suggested that the boys were autistic. Linda had to find out. When she told her husband Oscar that she would seek a diagnosis he resisted saying that his strict disciplinary actions would help the boys outgrow what he perceived to be challenging and disrespectful misbehavior. For the first time Linda acted without his permission.

Oscar lived in the old world of his Hispanic parents where obedience was the defining characteristic of good children. This was how he grew up. Discipline was enforced physically and decisively. Linda had played her part in this tradition by being passive and obedient herself even when her husband spanked the boys. But when the diagnosis was confirmed and she realized that her sons had a neurodevelopmental illness she felt empowered to intervene. Linda was relieved and felt in agreement with the diagnosis. Now she could get to work finding the help her sons needed. She believed completely in their intelligence and creativity. Both boys demonstrated incredible inventiveness with the arts, especially literature and story-making which they relished. What Linda dreaded was breaking the news to her husband.

The first thing I noticed when I met this family was how exhausted Linda was. It was hard to believe that she could continue day after day without respite given her fatigue. Developmentally both boys behaved younger than their actual ages of ten and twelve. Jose was staunchly protective of Joaquin and Joaquin looked up to his brother. Stunningly they honored the space each needed but with a cautious awareness of what was socially acceptable. Jose would caution Joaquin to restrain his rapid fire barrages of language in public and to stop flapping his hands. Joaquin would demur, lowering his head and then glance up shyly. Jose would then deliver a perfectly phrased speech that his brother clearly enjoyed. The love they demonstrated for each other was heartwarming but they had no other friends.

Linda told me that her husband sometimes hit the boys when they did not respond to him. He could not accept their differences and his disappointment in their development was communicated as blame. He insisted that they could change if they wanted to and that they were willfully refusing. Oscar felt ashamed of his sons. Linda was doing her best to soften his stern demeanor and invite his understanding. She believed in him too but the whole family was isolated.

Studies conducted by scientists at Trinity College Dublin and elsewhere have noted that childhood abuse can result in structural and functional brain changes. Stress and genetic variants can interact to change neurological development. (Science Daily 2010) Imaging technology provides the science that allows us to confirm that the abuse of children alters the anatomy of the developing brain. The limbic system is the part of the brain most vulnerable to adverse childhood experience. Repeated stress initiates hormonal flooding and elevations that dampen feedback mechanisms and lead to imbalances and dysregulation in the limbic systems, particularly the Hippocampus-Pituitary Axis (HPA).

While we may never know how much their father's actions shaped Jose's and Joaquin's neurodevelopment, we can posit that they played some role, if only by swirling the neurochemistry of

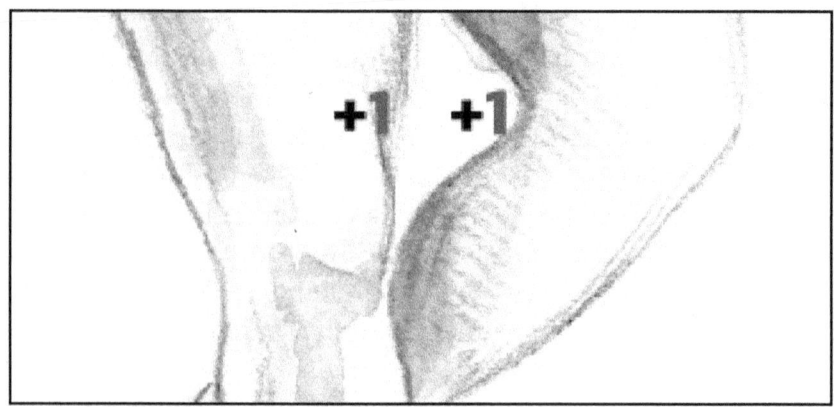

Figure 8.7 #1

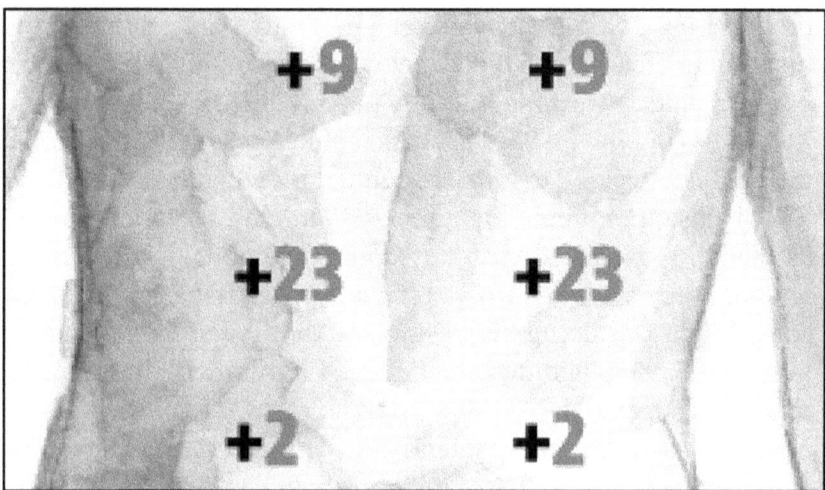

Figure 8.8 #23

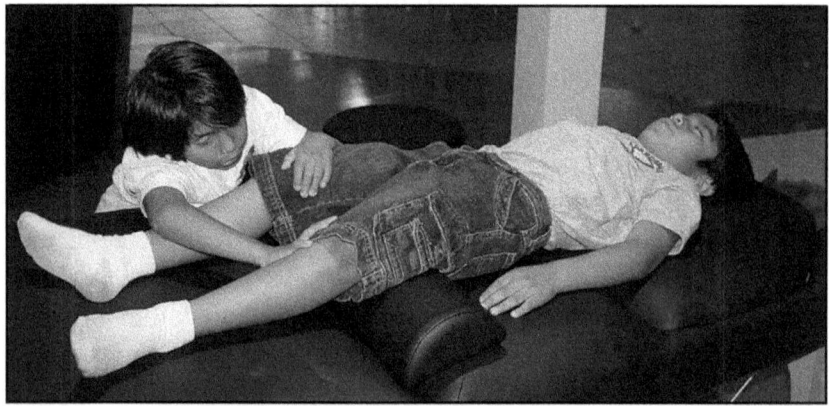

Figure 8.9 Palming #1 on the right and left sides.

trauma with that of autism. Using my whole family approach I engaged with everyone in this family to provide new options.

I began by providing Linda with regenerating self-care. She was the source of inspiration for the entire family. She gave selflessly to her husband and her sons out of her pure love for all of them. Because she was the driving force for the family and the navigator of its future I did not want her to be running on an empty tank. Parents of sensory needs children are frequently functioning on overload. Applied touch self-care can change that.

Both boys received multiple applied touch treatments that were designed to evoke their capacities to slow down. They liked being present for each other's sessions. While one received applied touch the other drew or read out loud. These boys had so much joy! The treatments that I created and that they learned to use for themselves were so effective and enjoyable that they began to treat each other. Site #1 (for grounding) and #23 (for adrenal regeneration) were their favorites.

Less than a month after a series of treatments the family received with me Linda wrote to tell me of significant changes in their lives. The most exciting news was that her sons were now demonstrating more awareness of the feelings of others. She described how they could be together, express affection, and comment on what they felt about each other and others. Linda told me that she often cried when they had these conversations and when the boys asked her why she was crying she would reply that she was shedding tears of joy because they were able to enjoy their family. The boys thrived in storytelling. They could translate their hyper-focus into detail and precise characterization. The boys' father relaxed once he saw that his sons could contain themselves. Though he was not as proactive as his wife, he stopped being an obstacle to healing. In fact he began to show some interest in the applied touch practices especially once he saw how they rejuvenated his wife. The last I heard he was considering using these for himself.

This family has become a model I can point to when enumerating the benefits of learning the TARA Approach to sensory integration and its components of applied touch as a form of family healing. They continue to this day to maintain home practices for regeneration and enhancing their innate intelligence and health.

The Magical Midline: Natalie's Story

Carolina is the single mother of two challenged girls. Natalie, her eldest, who was seven, had been diagnosed with atypical autism or PDD-NOS (Pervasive Developmental Disorder Not Otherwise Specified). Natalie's main struggle was with her tendency to dissociate. She appeared to go blank particularly in reciprocal social situations. She could not articulate her needs or her responses. This shifted dramatically whenever Natalie engaged in vigorous physical activity. She especially loved to swim. She emerged from the water vibrant and ready to engage but this would fade quickly until she swam again.

Carolina was a colleague of mine and a healthcare provider. We put our heads together and decided that the best thing we could do for this nine year old was to strengthen her midline. We reasoned that this was what was being stimulated when Natalie swam. In vigorous swimming, with her arms crossing her midline and her core engaged, she was empowered, centered and

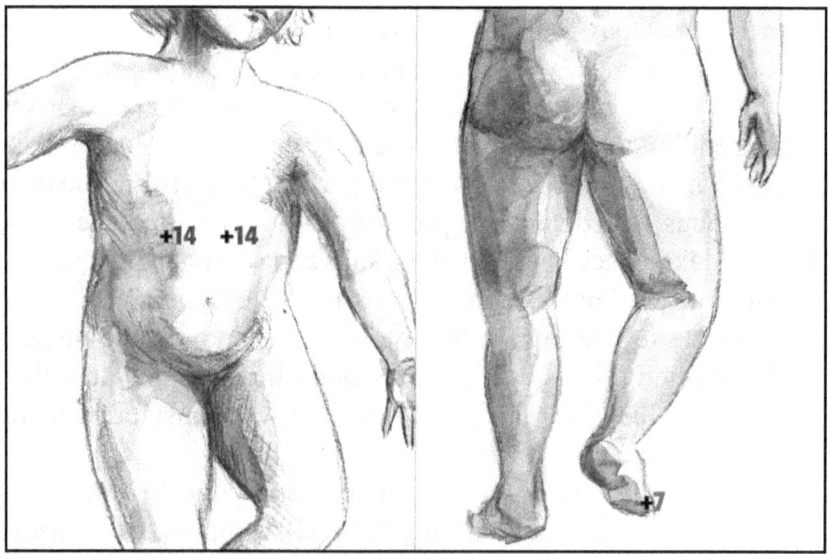

Figure 8.10 Holding Mid 14's and Both 7's

capable. We wanted her have that same experience on land and with people. I recommended that Carolina place the palm of one hand over both sites #14 on her daughter while grasping both #7's with her other hand. This is easy to do on a small child. Then I recommended that Natalie do the Diagonal Mediator release. This is an incredible brain hook-up that all children enjoy because it is such a balancing act. (See Figure 8.11)

Carolina suspected that another reason Natalie loved swimming was because mother and daughter had been swimming together since Natalie was under a year old. Carolina had been a champion swimmer in high school and college, a lifeguard and a swimming teacher for children. She got her girls in the water as soon as she could. We translated this to the possibility that Natalie would do better better with applied touch practices if she saw her mother modeling the interventions. We were betting on her mirror neuron system to kick in.

Every application listed below was done first by Carolina while Natalie watched. Of course her little sister, Eva, had to try the applications too! These three practiced strengthening their midline every

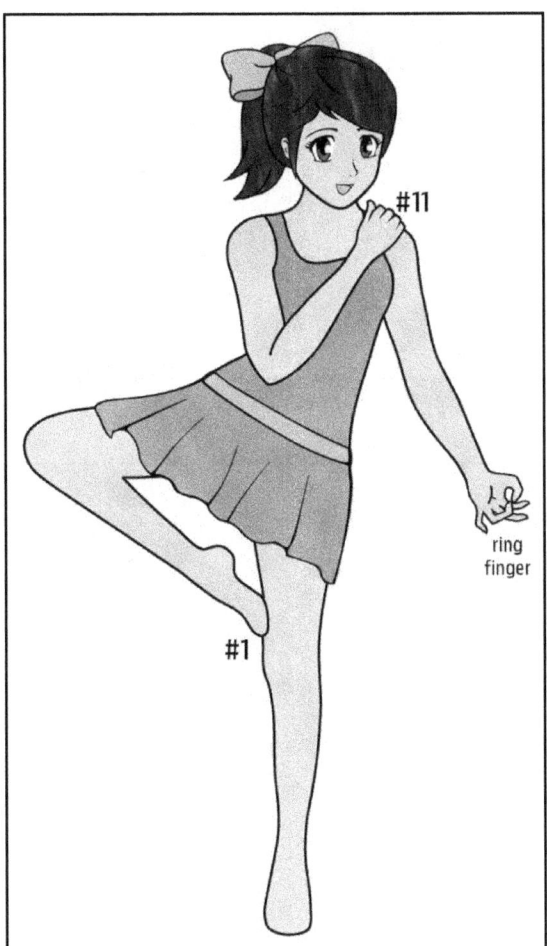

Figure 8.11 Diagonal Mediator Release

morning before school and before athletic activities. Everyone felt stronger as a result. The beauty of these applications is that they will provide benefit both generally and specifically. You can't go wrong.

Little by little, beginning after only two days of practicing this Midline Magic daily, Natalie began to come out of her shell. Everyone was thrilled to see more and more of this talented, vibrant

Figure 8.12 Palm Inju

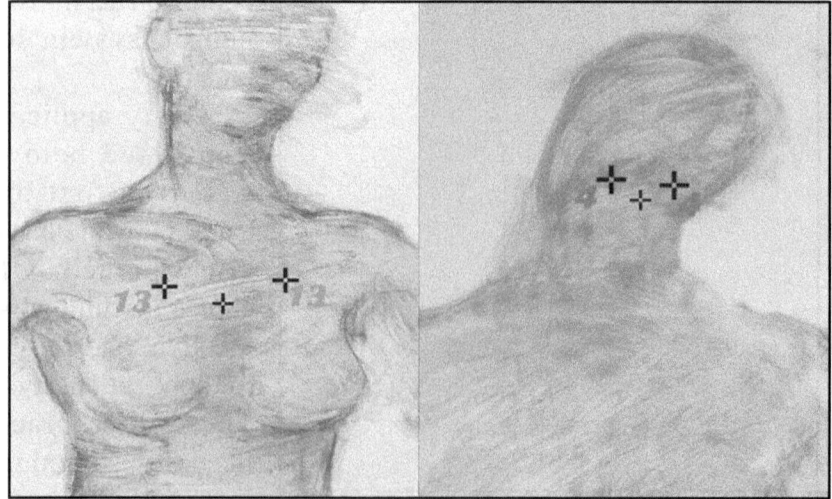

Figure 8.13 Holding Middle #13 and Middle #4

young being. To continue to deepen midline strength I added two more self-care practices. One is Palm Inju or the Prayer Posture (Figure 8.12). The other involves holding the center of the chest (middle #13) with the palm of one hand and the base of the occiput (middle #4) with the other. (See Figure 8.13)

Looking at the lives of families like these is like looking at magnificent landscapes. There are no television shows, movies or videos with characters that come close to having the power of these individuals to inspire me with their innocence, quest for the truth, love of their children and each other, and their daily dedication and perseverance. They are models for all of us and I am grateful to know them.

Summary: What These Family Stories Teach Us

1. Healing strategies for children are most successful in a family context.
2. The construction of a theory of mind for each child is a giant step in the direction of providing and implementing needed resources more effortlessly.
3. Trauma or abuse weaves a significant strand into the overall tapestry of sensory integration.
4. Culture, language, traditions and the developmental histories of both parents in a family are components in shaping the child's nervous system and sensory integration.
5. Stress and genetics always interact in brain development as do other environmental, epigenetic factors.
6. Parents and children alike, as well as healthcare providers, can implement effective interventions using applied touch.
7. Applied touch benefits parents so that they can be present and regenerated while facing the demands of advocating and caring for their neurodiverse children.
8. Parents need to resolve their intra- and interpersonal conflicts in a time and space allocated for them for this purpose. This allows them to be more effective in supporting the sensory integration of their children.
9. Treatment should always be guided or led by the child.

10. Creating harmony in the home environment contributes to sensory integration.
11. Parents and children are never to blame for sensory problems or autism.
12. Applied touch and limbic stimulation evoke innate healing responses and make daily life in families easier, more fluid and manageable.
13. Families can engage in fun therapeutic activities together to lessen anxiety and stress.
14. When family members join together to address sensory needs everyone grows and evolves.
15. The learning curve for families grappling with autism and sensory integration is steep but it builds the advocacy and leadership our children require.

End Notes

1. Cornwell, J. (2007). 'Master of Creation?' London Times Online, July 1, 2007.
2. Mines, Moriss and Persun 2012, inter alia, (in press).

McFadden, K.L. and Hernandez, T.D. (2010). 'Cardiovascular Benefits of Acupressure (Jin Shin) Following Stroke.' Complementary Therapies in Medicine 18, 4248.

McFadden, K.L., Healy, K.M., Dettmann, M.L., Kaye, J.T., Ito, T.A. and Hernandez, T.D. (2011) 'Acupressure as a Non-Pharmalogical Intervention for Traumatic Brain Injury (TBI).' Journal of Neurotrauma 28, 2134.

Chapter 1

3. Ayres A.J. (1964) 'Tactile functions, their relation to hyperactive and perceptual motor behavior.' American Journal of Occupational Therapy 18, pp. 611.
4. Prince Hughes, D. (2004) 'Songs of the Gorilla Nation: My Journey Through Autism.' New York: Crown Publishing Group, p. 15 and throughout early chapters.
5. Prince Hughes, D. (2004) 'Songs of the Gorilla Nation: My Journey Through Autism.' New York: Crown Publishing Group, p. 35.
6. Schneider M.L., Moore C.F., Gajewski L.L., Larson J.A., Roberts A.D., Converse A.K., and DeJesus O.T. (2008) 'Sensory Processing Disorder in a Primate Model: Evidence From a Longitudinal Study of Prenatal Alcohol and Prenatal Stress Effects.' Child Development 79, Number 1, pp. 106-108.
7. Samuels, N. (March 2, 2013) Personal Correspondence.
8. Samuels, N. (March 2, 2013) Personal Correspondence.
9. Smith, K. and Gouze, K. (2004 & 2010) 'The Sensory Sensitive Child: Practical Solutions for Out of Bounds Behavior.' New York: HarperCollins Publishers, Inc.
10. Ackerman, D. (2011) 'A Natural History of the Senses.' New York: Knopf Doubleday Publishing Group, p. 1.
11. Ermer, J. and Dunn, W. (1998) 'The Sensory Profile: A Discriminant Analysis of Children With and Without Disabilities.' The American Journal of Occupational Therapy 52, 4, 287.

Chapter 2

12. Cozolino, L. (2006) 'The Neuroscience of Human Relationships: Attachment and the Developing Brain.' New York: W. W. Norton & Company, Inc., p. 43.

13. Mines, Morris and Persun 2012, inter alia, (in press).

14. Karr-Morse, R. and Wiley, M.S. (2012) 'Sacred Sick: The Role of Childhood Trauma in Adult Disease.' New York: Basic Books., p. 201.

15. Solomon, A. (2012) 'Far From the Tree: Parents, Children and the Search for Identity.' New York: Scribner, p.257.

Chapter 3

16. Fleischmann, A. (2012) 'Carly's Voice: Breaking Through Autism.' New York: Simon and Schuster, p. 101.

17. Robinson, J.E. (2007 & 2008) 'Look Me in the Eye: My Life with Asperger's.' New York: Three Rivers Press.

18. Fleischmann 2012.

19. Fleischmann 2012, p. 115.

20. Cacioppo, J.T. and Patrick, W. (2008) 'Loneliness: Human Nature and the Need for Social Connection.' New York: W. W. Norton & Company. Inter alia but also see, for example, pp. 12, 34, and 141.

21. Henry, D.P., Zdenek, D., and Zdenek, M. (2003) 'Born Unwanted. Observations from the Prague Study.' American Psychological Association 58, 5, 224229.

Chapter 4

22. Kelly, M. (2004, first published 1999) 'The Rhythm of Life: Living Every Day with Passion and Purpose.' New York: Fireside, p. 82.

23. Solomon, A. (2012) 'Far From the Tree: Parents, Children and the Search for Identity.' New York: Scribner, inter alia.

24. Tammet, Daniel (2006) 'Born On A Blue Day: Inside the Extraordinary Mind of an Autistic Savant.' New York: Free Press, a Division of Simon & Schuster, Inc.

Tammet, Daniel (2009) 'Embracing the Wide Sky: A Tour Across the Horizons of the Mind.' New York: Free Press, a Division of Simon & Schuster, Inc.

25. Cozolino 2006, p. 284.

26. Roelfsema, M.T., Hoekstra, R.A., Allison, C., Wheelwright, S., Brayne, C., et al (2012) 'Are Autism Spectrum Conditions More Prevalent in an

Information-Technology Region? A School Based Study of Three Regions in the Netherlands.' Journal of Autism and Developmental Disorders, DOI: 10.1007/s1080301113021.

27. (Rice 2009, pp 1-20)
28. Baron-Cohen, S. (2011) 'The Science of Evil: On Empathy and the Origins of Cruelty.' New York: Basic Books, p. 37.
29. Moburg, K.U. (2003) 'The Oxytocin Factor: Tapping the Hormone of Calm, Love, and Healing.' Massachusetts: Perseus Books Group. (Original work published in 200).
30. Baron-Cohen 2011, p. 37.
31. Fleischmann 2012, p. 121133.
32. Fleischmann 2012, p. 191.

Chapter 5

33. Miller, L.J. (2006) 'Sensational Kids: Hope and Help for Children with Sensory Processing Disorder (SPD).' New York: Penguin Books, p. 20.
34. McFadden, K.L., Healy, K.M., Dettmann, M.L., Kaye, J.T., Ito, T.A., and Hernandez, T.D. (2011) 'Acupressure as a Non-Pharmacological Intervention for Traumatic Brain Injury (TBI).' Journal of Neurotrauma 28, 2134.

McFadden, K. L. and Hernandez, T. D. (2010) 'Cardiovascular Benefits of Acupressure (Jin Shin) Following Stroke.' Complementary Therapies in Medicine 18, 4248.

35. LN, Mother of Two Boys in Oklahoma — Personal Testimony
36. Miller 2006, p. 245.
37. Mines, Morris and Persun 2012, inter alia, (in press).

Chapter 6

38. Cornwell, J. (2007) 'Master of Creation?' London Times Online, July 1, 2007.
39. Mines, S., Morris, T. and Persun, D. (2012) 'The Effect of Applied Touch on Behavior of Autistic Children.' Inter alia, (in press).
40. Teresa, M. (2001, first pusblished 1995) 'No Greater Love.' California: New World Library, p. 94.
41. Solomon, A. (2012) 'Far From the Tree: Parents, Children and the Search for Identity.' New York: Schibner, pp. 37, 43.
42. Grandin, T. (2011) 'The Way I See It, Revised and Expanded 2nd Edition: A Personal Look at Autism and Asperger's.' Texas: Future Horizons, Inc., p. 35.

43. Likens, A. (2012) 'Finding Kansas: Living and Decoding Asperger's Syndrome.' New York: Penguin.
44. Powers, R. (2005) 'Mark Twain: A Life.' New York: Simon and Schuster, p. 8.
45. Natenshon, A.H. and Toomey, K. (2012) 'Feeding Disorders and Picky Eating in Infants and Children, Treating Eating disorders.com.'
46. American Academy of Pediatrics Study.
47. Natenshon and Toomey, 2012, p. 134.
48. Ianco, I., Cohen, E., Yehuda, Y.B. and Kotler, M. (2006) 'Treatment of eating disorders improves eating symptoms but not alexithymia and dissociation proneness.' Comprehensive Psychiatry, May June 4y, 3, 189193.
49. Beat (2010) Survey. Accessed at http://www.beat.co.uk/.
50. Mines, Morris, and Persun 2012, inter alia, in press.
51. Lowry, K. (2008) 'The Seventh Inning Sit: A Journey of ADHD.' Kindle e-book, p. 21.
52. Moore, R. (1991) 'Awakening the Hidden Storyteller.' Boston: Shambhala, p. 19.

Chapter 7

53. Tammet ~ Whether speaking on YouTube or in the UK's Guardian or The Scotsman, or in any of his books, Daniel Tammet's interviews all spread the message of the health and power of neurodiversity and the benefits of not only tolerance and acceptance but of welcoming difference.
54. Emery, M.J. (2004) 'Art Therapy as an Intervention for Autism.' Journal of the American Art Therapy Association 21, 3, 143147.
55. Emery 2004, p. 147.
56. Becker, L. (1983) 'With Eyes Wide Open.' Documentary Film.
57. Leishman, M. (1958) 'Richard Wawro.' Accessed at http://www.wawro.net/molly_leishmans_story.html.
58. American Dance Therapy Association (2009). Accessed at http://www.adta.org/.
59. Grandin ~ Temple Grandin's YouTube videos, including her interview with Rupert Isaacs on who created the Horse Boy Foundation, reiterate her connection with animals in general and with horses in specific. She openly declares her affinity, connection and love of horses.
60. Campbell, D. (2009) 'The Mozart Effect for Children.' New York: Harper Collins. (Original work published in 2000), p. 37.

61. Campbell, D. (2009) 'The Mozart Effect for Children.' New York: Harper Collins. (Original work published in 2000), p. 32.
62. Gardner, H. (1983) 'Frames of Mines: The Theory of Multiple Intelligences.' New York: Basic Book
63. Gardner 1983
64. Yeats 2010, p. 49.
65. Yeats 2010
66. Mines, S. (2003) 'We Are In Shock: How Overwhelming Experiences Shatter You And What You Can Do About It.' New Jersey: Career Press, Inc., p. 196.
67. Mines, S. (1998) 'The Dreaming Child: How Children Can Help Themselves Recover From Illness & Injury.' Boulder, Colorado: The Dom Project, pp. 25.
68. Ball, M. All quotes, books and references to Marshall Ball come from his two websites: www.marshallball.com or www.throughfulhouse.org.
69. Fleischmann, C. (2012) 'Carly's Blog.' Accessed at www.carlysvoice.com/home/aboutcarly.
70. Ball, M.S. and Ball, T. (1999) 'Kiss of God: The Wisdom of a Silent Child.' Florida: Health Communications, Inc.
71. Landa, R. (2012) Personal Correspondence.
72. Vonder Hulls, D.S., Walker, L.K., Powell, J.M. (2006) 'Clinicians' perceptions of the benefits of aquatic therapy for young children with autism: a preliminary study.' Physical, Occupational Therapy Pediatricsr. 26, 12, 1322.
73. Hall, E. (2010) 'Now I See the Moon: A Mother, A Son, A Miracle.' New York: HarperCollins Publishers, Inc., p. 273.
74. American Speech Language Hearing Association (2011). Accessed at http://www.asha.org/About/news/PressRelease/2011/DoTheaterExperiencesIncreaseSocialSkillsForStudentsWithAutism.
75. Keller, H. (2005) Helen Keller Foundation at http://www.helenkellerfoundation.org/about_HK.asp
76. Issacson, W. and Baker, D. (2011) 'Steve Jobs.' New York: Simon & Schuster
77. ONE News (2011) 'Software promises access for the blind and deaf.' Source: ONE News. Accessed at http://tvnz.co.nz/technologynews/softwarepromisesaccessblindanddeaf4666133.
78. ONE News (2011).

79. Field, T. (2003, first published 2001) 'Touch.' Cambridge: Bradford Books, p. 77.
80. Mines, Morris and Persun 2012, inter alia, (in press).
81. Young A. (2010) 'Autism: From the Traditional Chinese Medicine Perspective, Keefer Michael.'
82. Finando, D. (2008) 'Acupoint and Trigger Point Therapy for Babies and Children: A Parent's Healing Touch.' Vermont: Healing Arts Press.
83. Porges, S.W. (2004) 'The Vagus: A Mediator of Behavioral and Physiologic Features Associated with Autism.' Bauman, M.L. and Kemper, T.L. (eds), The Neurobiology of Autism. Baltimore: Johns Hopkins University Press.
84. Mines, Morris and Persun 2012, inter alia, (in press).
85. Mines, S. (2010) 'Special Needs Children 11 Elements of Integrative Bodywork.' Massage & Bodywork September/October 2012, 3443.
86. The Center for AAC & Autism (2009). Accessed at http://www.aacandautism.com/why-aac.
87. Mooney, J. (2011) 'Neurodiversity: A Compass to a Changing World.' YouTube: Conference on Inclusive Education. Accessed at http://www.youtube.com/watch?v=srWWMVKG56M.
88. Mooney, J. (2007) 'The Short Bus A Journey Beyond Normal.' New York: Henry Holt and Company, LLC.
89. Hartmann, T. and Palladino, L.J. (2005) 'The Edison Gene: ADHD and the Gift of the Hunter Child.' Vermont: Park Street Press.
90. Lowry 2008, inter alia.
91. Campbell, D. (2009) 'The Mozart Effect for Children.' New York: Harper Collins. (Original work published in 2000), p.
92. Mooney (2011).
93. Perry, B., and Szalavitz, M. (2011) 'Born For Love: Why Empathy is Essential — and Endangered.' New York: HarperCollins Publishers, p. 230.
94. Landrigan, Lambertini and Birnbaum 2012
95. Healy, J.M. (2004). 'Your Child's Growing Mind: Brain Development and Learning From Birth to Adolescence.' New York: Broadway Books. (Original work published in 1987), p. 164.
96. Jones, H. (2012) Personal Correspondence.
97. Mines, Morris and Persun 2012, inter alia, (in press).
98. Finando 2008, p. 160.
99. Mother of boy with autism — Personal Correspondence.
100. Gerber, T. (2012) Personal Correspondence.

101. Sensory Processing Disorder (2012). Accessed at http://www.sensory-processingdisorder.com/weightedblankets.html.
102. Biel, L. and Peske, N. (2009) 'Raising A Sensory Smart Child: The Definitive Handbook for Helping Your Child with Sensory Processing Issues.' New York: Penguin, pp. 113116.
103. Grandin, T. (1995 & 2006) 'Thinking in Pictures: My Life with Autism.' New York: Vintage Books, a Division of Random House, Inc., p. 62.
104. Art Dyslexia Trust (ADT) (2011) Art Dyslexia Trust. Accessed at http://www.artdyslexiatrust.ord/node/7.
105. Schneider, M. (1998) 'Self-Healing: My Life and Vision.' New York: Penguin.
106. Benoit, R. and Benoit, J. (2010) 'Jillian's Story: How Vision Therapy Changed My Daughter's Life.' Texas: The Small Press.
107. Schneider (2010) 'Meir Schneider My Life and Vision.' YouTube: Interview by Iain McNay. Accessed at http://www.youtube.com/watch?v=OmwtKt5TwNs.
108. Grandin 1995 & 2006, p. 79.

Chapter 8

109. Baniel, A. (2012) 'Kids Beyond Limits.' New York: Penguin, p. 77.
110. Solomon, A. (2012) 'Far From the Tree: Parents, Children and the Search for Identity.' New York: Scribner, p. 53.
111. Science Daily (2010) 'Childhood Stress Such as Abuse or Emotional Neglect Can Result in Structural Brain Changes.' Dublin: Trinity College.

Bibliography

Adler, J. (2006) 'Presence: From Autism to the Discipline of Authentic Movement an Address by Janet Adler.' *Contact Quarterly Summer/Fall* 2006, 11-17.

Andersen, H.C. (2004) *True Story of My Life, translated by Mary Howitt in 1847*, Project Gutenberg. Accessed on 2011 at http://www.gutenberg.org/dirs/etext04/7hcan10.txt.

Andersen, H.C. (2006) *Stories from Hans Christian Andersen*, Project Gutenberg. Accessed on 2011 at http://www.gutenberg.org/files/17860/17860-h/17860-h.htm.

Attwood, T. (2007 & 2008) *The Complete Guide to Asperger's Syndrome*. London: Jessica Kingsley Publishers.

Auer, C. and M. (2010) *Making Sense of Your Senses*. Oakland: New Harbinger.

Badenoch, B. (2008) *Being a Brain-Wise Therapist: A Practical Guide to Interpersonal Neurobiology.* New York: W.W. Norton & Company, Inc.

Baron-Cohen, S., Cosmides, L. and Tooby, J. (1997) *Mindblindness: An Essay on Autism and Theory of Mind.* MIT Press.

Belis, T. J. (2003) *When the Brain Can't Hear: Unraveling The Mystery of Auditory Processing Disorder.* New York: Atria Books. (Original work published 2002).

Boyden, E. and DE Gabrieli, J., Ghosh, S. 'Using Oxytocin to Improve Social Cognition in Participants with Autism Spectrum Disorder.'

Brown, D. and Brown, D. (2010) *A Wizard from the Start: The Incredible Boyhood and Amazing Inventions of Thomas Edison.* New York: Houghton Mifflin Harcourt Publishing Company.

Brown, J. (2010) *Writers on the Spectrum: How Autism and Asperger Syndrome Have Influenced Literary Writing*, Kindle ebook.

Brown, R.P. and Gerbarg, P.L. (2012) *Non Drug Treatments for ADHD: New Options for Kids, Adults and Clinicians.* New York: Norton

Carnahan, C., Musti-Rao, S., and Bailey, J. (2009) 'Promoting active engagement in small group learning experiences for students with autism and significant learning needs. (Report).' Education & Treatment of Children. West Virginia University Press. *High Beam Research.*

Causton-Theoharis, J., Ashby, C., and Cosier, M. (2009) 'Islands of Loneliness: Exploring Social Interaction Through the Autobiographies of Individuals With Autism.' *Intellectual and Developmental Disabilities 47*, 2, 84-96.

Circle of One (2000) *Testimony of John E. Upledger, D.O., O.M.M. Before the Committee on Government Reform U.S. House of Representatives. An Etiologic Model for Autism.* Accessed at

Cohen, K. (2011) *Seeing Ezra: A Mother's Story of Autism, Unconditional Love, and the Meaning of Normal.* Berkeley: Seal Press.

Dickinson, E. (2003) *The Collected Poems of Emily Dickinson, Introduction and Notes by Rachel Wetzsteo.*, New York: First Creative Media.

J. W. (2004) 'The Social Engagement System: Functional Differences in Individuals with Autism.'

Edelman, G.M. (1992) *Bright Air, Brilliant Fire: On The Matter Of The Mind.* New York: Basic Books

Edelman, G.M. (2004) *Wider than the Sky: The Phenomenal Gift of Consciousness.* United States of America: Yale University Press.

Escalona, A., Field, T., Singer-Strunck, R., Cullen, C., Hartshorn, K. (2001) 'Brief report: improvements in the behavior of children with autism following massage therapy.' *Journal of Autism Developmental Disorders 31*, 5, 513-516.

Fetters, L. and Kluzik, J. (1996) 'The Effects of Neurodevelopmental Treatment Versus Practice on the Reaching of Children With Spastic Cerebal Palsy.' *Physical Therapy 76*, 4, 346-358.

Fitzgerald, M., O'Brian, B. and McBride, K. (2007) *Genius Genes: How Asperger Talents Changed the World.* Kansas: Autism Asperger Publishing Company.

Fitzgerald, M. (2003) *Autism and Creativity*, Brunner-Routledge.

Fitzgerald, M. (2005) *The Genesis of Artistic Creativity: Asperger's Syndrome And The Arts.* London: Jessica Kingsley Publishers.

Fitzgerald, M. and Corvin, A. (2001) *Diagnoses and differential diagnosis of Aspergers syndrome.* Advances in Psychiatric Treatment, DOI: 10.1192/apt.7.4.310.

Fitzgerald, M. and Walker, A. (2006) *Unstoppable Brilliance: Irish Geniuses and Asperger's Syndrome.* Dublin: Liberties Press.

Gardner H. (1993) *Multiple Intelligences: The Theory in Practice.* New York: Basic Books.

Gardner H. (2000) *Intelligence Reframed: Multiple Intelligences for the 21st Century.* New York: Basic Books.

Grandin, T. (2008) *Humane Livestock Handling: Understanding livestock behavior and building facilities for healthier animals.* Massachusetts: Storey Publishing.

Grandin, T. and Barron, S. (2005) *The Unwritten Rules of Social Relationships: Decoding Social Mysteries Through the Unique Perspectives of Autism.* Texas: Future Horizons, Inc.

Grandin, T. and Duffy, K. (2008) *Developing Talents: Careers For Individuals With Asperger Syndrome And High-functioning Autism- Updated, Expanded Edition.* Kansas: Autism Asperger Publishing Company.

Grandin, T. and Johnson, C. (2005) *Animals in Translation: Using the Mysteries of Autism to Decode Animal Behavior.* New York: Scribner.

Grandin, T. and Johnson, C. (2009) *Animals Make Us Human: Creating the Best Life for Animals.* Florida: Houghton Mifflin Harcourt Publishing Company.

Grandin, T. and Scariano, M.M. (1986) *Emergence: Labeled Autistic,* California: Arena Press.

Hendricks, S. (2010) *The Adolescent and Adult Neurodiversity Handbook.* London: Jessica Kingsley Publishers.

Hernandez, T. D., McFadden, K. L., Ivankovich, B. G., Gavito, C., Huerta, S. Effects of jin shin on motor function following stroke (abstract). JINS. 2007; 13, Suppl S1. DOI: 10.1017/S1355617707079969:http://journals.cambridge.org/action/displayIssue? jid=INS&volumeID=13&issueID=S 11.

Hernandez, T. D., McFadden, K. L., Ivankovich, B. G., Gavito, C., Huerta, S. (2007) 'Functional improvement after stroke: A role for complementary medicine.' *Journal of Neuropsychiatry and Clinical Neuroscience, 19*, 213.

Hernandez, T. D., Ramsberger, G., Kurland, J., Hadler, B. (2003) 'Functional consequences of jin shin tara treatment after stroke: a preliminary investigation.' *Society for Acupuncture Research Abstracts* 43.

Hoopes, A. M. (2009) *Eye Power: An Updated Report on Vision Therapy.* London: Jessica Kingsley Publishers.

Isaacson, W. (2007) *Einstein: His Life and Universe.* New York: Simon & Schuster.

Kaplan, M. (2005) *Seeing Through New Eyes: Changing the Lives of Children with Autism, Asperger's Syndrome and Other Developmental Disabilities with Vision Therapy.* London: Jessica Kingsley Publishers.

Kelland, K. (2012) *Talking Things Through in Your Head May Help Autism,* Development and Psychopathology, source: http://bit.ly/wOazFh.

Landrigan, P.J., Lambertini, L. and Birnbaum, L.S. (2012) *A Research Strategy to Discover the Environmental Causes of Autism and Neurodevelopmental Disabilities.* Environ Health Perspect 120:a258-a260. http://dx.doi.org/10.1289/ehp.1104285.

Lee, M. S., Kim, J. I., Ernst, E. (2011) 'Massage therapy for children with autism spectrum disorders: a systematic review.' *Journal of Clinical Psychiatry 72*, 3, 406-411.

Lovett, J. (2005) *Solutions for Adults with Asperger Syndrome: Maximizing the Benefits, Minimizing the Drawbacks to Achieve Success.* Massachusetts: Fair Winds Press.

Loving, J. (2010) *Mark Twain: The Adventures of Samuel L. Clemens.* Berkeley: University of California Press.

Madaule, P. (1994) *When Listening Comes Alive: A Guide to Effective Learning and Communication.* Toronto: The Listening Centre.

Mauro, T. and Cermak, S.A. (2006) *The Everything Parent's Guide To Sensory Integration Disorder: Get the Right Diagnosis, Understand Treatments, And Advocate for Your Child.* Massachusetts: Adams Media, an F & W Company.

McCollum, D. (2006) *Child Maltreatment and Brain Development.* Minnesota: Clinical and Health Affairs Minnesota Medicine.

Medical Press (2012) *New study confirms that mom's love good for child's brain.* Psychology and Psychiatry, http://medicalexpress.com/news/2012-01-mom-good-child-brain.html.

Millan, A. (2010) *Autism-Believe in the Future: From Infancy to Independence*, Indiana: iUniverse.

Miller, A. (2007) *The Drama of the Gifted Child: The Search for the True Self.* New York: Basic Books. (Original work published in German in 1979).

Montgomery, S. and Grandin, T. (2012) *Temple Grandin: How the Girl Who Loved Cows Embraced Autism and Changed the World.* New York: Houghton Mifflin Harcourt Publishing Company.

Morvay, B. (2010) *My Brother is Different: A sibling's guide to coping with Autism*, Kindle ebook.

Neider, C. (eds) (1996) *The Autobiography of Mark Twain.* New York: Harper.

Piravej, K., Tangtrongchitr, P., Chandarasiri, P., Paothong, L., Sukprasong, S. (2009) 'Effects of Thai traditional massage on autistic children's behavior.' *Journal of Alternative Complementary Medicine 15*, 12, 1355-1361.

Porges, S.W. (2006) 'The Polyvagal Perspective.' *Biological Psychology 74*, (2007) 116-143.

Press, L. J. and Richman, J. E. (2009) 'The Role of Optometry in Early Identification of Autism Spectrum Disorder.' *Optometry & Vision Development 40*, 3, 141-149.

Prupas, A., Harvey, W. J., and Benjamin, J. (2006) 'Research: Early Intervention Aquatics: A Program for Children with Autism and their Families.' *Journal of Physical Education, Recreation & Dance 77*, 2, 46-51.

Ruben, S. (2010) *Awakening Ashley: Mozart Knocks Autism on Its Ear.* Indiana: iUniverse. (Original work published 2004).

Sacks, O. (1996) *An Anthropologist on Mars: Seven Paradoxical Tales.* Kindle Book.

Sacks, O. (1998) *The Island of the Colorblind.* New York: Vintage Books.

Sacks, O. (1998) *The Man Who Mistook His Wife for a Hat.* New York: Touchstone. (Original work published in 1970).

Sacks, O. (1999) *Awakenings.* New York: Vintage Books. (Original work published in 1973).

Sacks, O. (1999) *Migraine.* New York: Vintage Books. (Original work published in 1992).

Sacks, O. (2000) *Seeing Voices.* New York: Vintage Books. (Original work Published in 1989).

Sacks, O. (2002) *Uncle Tungsten: Memories of a Chemical Boyhood.* Kindle Book.

Sacks, O. (2008) *Musicophilia: Tales of Music and the Brain, Revised and Expanded Edition.* New York: Vintage Books. (Original work published in 2007).

Sacks, O. (2011) *The Mind's Eye.* New York: Vintage Books. (Original work published in 2010).

Santomauro, J. (eds) (2012) *Autism All Stars.* London: Jessica Kingsley Publishers.

Sell, C. (editor) (2007) *A Cup of Comfort for Parents of Children with Autism: Stories of Hope and Everyday Success.* Massachusetts: Adams Media, an F&W Company.

Sher, B. (2009) *Early Intervention Games: Fun, Joyful Ways to Develop Social and Motor Skills in Children with Autism Spectrum or Sensory Processing Disorders.* San Francisco: Jossey-Bass.

Siegel, D.J. (1999) *The Developing Mind: Toward a Neurobiology of Interpersonal Experience.* New York: Guilford Press.

Siegel, D.J. (2007) *The Mindful Brain: Reflections and Attunement in the Cultivation of Well-Being.* New York: W.W. Norton & Company, Inc.

Siegel, D. J. (2010) *Mindsight: The New Science of Personal Transformation.* Bantum.

Siegel, D. J. (2012) The Developing Mind: *How Relationships and the Brain Interact to Shape Who We Are.* New York: Guilford Press.

Siegel, D. J. and Hartzell, M. (2003) *Parenting From the Inside Out.* Tarcher.

Silva, L. M., Schalock, M., Ayres, R., Bunse, C., Budden, S. (2009) 'Qigong massage treatment for sensory and self-regulation problems in young children with autism: a randomized controlled trial.' *American Journal of Occupational Therapy 63*, 4, 423-432.

Simon, R. (2002 & 2003) *Riding the Bus with my Sister: A True Life Journey.* New York: Houghton-Mifflin.

Smart, T. (2010) *The Power of Neurodiversity.* Philadelphia: DaCapo.

Smith, H. E. (eds) (2010) *Autobiography of Mark Twain.* The Mark Twain Project, a publication program of the Bancroft Library.

Smith, K. and Gouze, K. (2004 & 2010) *The Sensory Sensitive Child: Practical Solutions for Out-of-Bounds Behavior.* New York: HarperCollins Publishers, Inc.

Snowling, M. (2006) *Dyslexia.* Blackwell.

Stehli, A. (2010) *The Sound of Falling Snow: Stories of Recovery from Autism and Related Disorders.* Georgiana Publishing.

Sutton, A.A. (1996) 'The Basis for Visual Development from Prenatal Through Infancy.' *Journal of Optometric Vision Development 27*, 80-86.

Totora, S. (2005) *The Dancing Dialogue: Using the Communicative Power of Movement with Young Children.* Baltimore: Brookes.

Walton, S. (2010) *Coloring Outside Autism's Lines: 50+ Activities, Adventures, and Celebrations for Families with Children with Autism,* Illinois: Sourcebooks, Inc.

References

American Dance Therapy Association (2009) Accessed at http://www.adta.org/.

American Speech-Language-Hearing Association (1997-2011) Accessed at http://www.asha.org/About/news/Press-Release/2011/Do-Theater-Experiences-Increase-Social

Skills-For-Students-With-Autsm .

Arts Dyslexia Trust (ADT) (2011) Art Dyslexia Trust. Accessed at http://www.artsdyslexiatrust.org/node/7.

Autism National Committee (2007) **'The Combating Autism Act of 2006'** *The Communicator 15*, 1.

Ball, M. (1998) All quotes, books and references to Marshall Ball come from his two websites: www.marshallball.com or www.thoughfulhouse.org.

Ball, M.S. and Ball, T. (1999) *Kiss of God: The Wisdom of a Silent Child*. Florida: Health Communications, Incorporated.

Baniel, A. (2012) *Kids Beyond Limits*. New York: Penguin.

Baron-Cohen, S. (2011) *The Science of Evil: On Empathy and the Origins of Cruelty*. New York: Basic Books.

B-eat (2010) *Survey*. Accessed at http://www.b-eat.co.uk/.

Benoit, R. and Benoit, J. (2010) *Jillian's Story: How Vision Therapy Changed My Daughter's Life*. Texas: The Small Press.

Biel, L. and Peske, N. (2009) *Raising A Sensory Smart Child: The Definitive Handbook for Helping Your Child with Sensory Processing Issues*. New York: Penguin.

Cacioppo, J. T. and Patrick, W. (2008) *Loneliness: Human Nature and the Need for Social Connection*. New York: W. W. Norton & Company.

Campell, D. (2009) *The Mozart Effect*. New York: HarperCollins. (Original work published in 1997).

Campbell, D. (2009) *The Mozart Effect for Children*. New York: HarperCollins. (Original work published in 2000), p. 37.

Children's Therapeutics of Autism (2012). Accessed at http://www.childrenstherapeutics.com/therainterv/NeurodevelopmentalTreeatment.php

Cornwell, J. (2007) *'Master of Creation?'* London Times Online.

Cozolino, L. (2006) *The Neuroscience of Human Relationships: Attachment and the*

Developing Brain. New York: W. W. Norton & Company, Inc.

Cutler, E. (2004) *A Thorn in My Pocket: Temple Grandin's Mother Tells the Family Story.* Arlington: Future Horizons.

Emery, M.J. (2004) 'Art Therapy as an Intervention for Autism.' *Journal of the American Art Therapy Association 21*, 3, 143-147.

Eide, B. L. and Eide, F. F. (2012) *The Dyslexic Advantage: Unlocking the Hidden Potential of the Dyslexic Brain.* New York: Plume.

Field, T. (2003, first published 2001) *Touch.* Cambridge: Bradford Books, p. 77.

Finando, D. (2008) *Acupoint and Trigger Point Therapy for Babies and Children: A Parent's Healing Touch.* Vermont: Healing Arts Press.

Fleischmann, A. (2012) *Carly's Voice: Breaking Through Autism.* New York: Simon and Schuster.

Fleischmann, C. (2012) Carly's Blog. Accessed at www.carlysvoice.com/home/aboutcarly.

Gardner, H. (1983) *Frames of Mind: The Theory of Multiple Intelligences.* New York: Basic Books.

Grandin, T. (1995 & 2006) *Thinking in Pictures: My Life with Autism.* New York: Vintage Books, a Division of Random House, Inc., p. 79.

Grandin, T. (2011) *The Way I See It, Revised and Expanded 2nd Edition: A Personal Look at Autism and Asperger's.* Texas: Future Horizons, Inc., p. 35.

Habegger, A. (2001) *My Wars Are Laid in Books: The Life of Emily Dickenson.* New York: Modern Library a division of Random House, Inc., p. 12.

Hadden, M. (2006) *The Talking Horse and the Sad Girl and the Village Under the Sea: Poems.* New York: Vintage Books.

Hall, E. (2010) *Now I See the Moon: A Mother, a Son, a Miracle.* New York: HarperCollins Publishers, Inc.

Hartmann, T. and Palladino, L. J. (2005) *The Edison Gene: ADHD and the Gift of the Hunter Child.* Vermont: Park Street Press.

Healy, J. M. (2004) *Your Child's Growing Mind: Brain Development and Learning From Birth to Adolescence.* New York: Broadway Books. (Original work published in 1987).

Henry, D.P., Zdenek, D., and Zdenek, M. (2003) 'Born Unwanted. Observations from the Prague Study.' *American Psychological Association 58*, 5, 224-229.

Ianco, I., Cohen, E., Yehuda, Y.B. and Kotler, M. (2006) 'Treatment of eating disorders improves eating symptoms but not alexithymia and dissociation proneness.' *Compr Psychiatry May-June 4y,* 3, 189-93.

Isaacson, W. and Baker, D. (2011) *Steve Jobs.* New York: Simon & Schuster.

Keller, Helen (2005) *Helen Keller Education.* Helen Keller Foundation. Accessed at http://www.helenkellerfoundation.org/education.asp.

Leishman, M. (1958) *Richard Wawro.* Accessed at http://www.wawro.net/molly_leishmans_story.html

Likens, A. (2012) *Finding Kansas: Living and Decoding Asperger's Syndrome.* New York: Penguin.

Lowry, K. (2008) *The Seventh Inning Sit: A Journey of ADHD*, Karen Lowry.

Margerison, C. (2011) *Meet Thomas Edison - An eStory: Inspirational Stories.* England: Viewpoint Resources, Ltd.

McFadden, K. L. and Hernandez, T. D. (2010) 'Cardiovascular Benefits of Acupressure (Jin Shin) Following Stroke.' *Complementary Therapies in Medicine 18*, 42-48.

McFadden, K. L., Healy, K. M., Dettmann, M. L., Kaye, J. T., Ito, T. A. and Hernandez, T. D. (2011) 'Acupressure as a Non-Pharmacological Intervention for Traumatic Brain Injury (TBI).' *Journal of Neurotrauma 28*, 21-34.

Miller, L. J. (2006) *Sensational Kids: Hope and Help for Children with Sensory Processing Disorder (SPD).* New York: Penguin Books, p. 245 & 254.

Miner, M. and Siegel, L.S. (1992) 'William Butler Yeats: dyslexic?' *Journal of Learning Disabilities 25*, 6, 372-375.

Mines, S. (1998) *The Dreaming Child: How Children Can Help Themselves Recover From Illness & Injury.* Boulder, Colorado: The Dom Project.

Mines, S. (2003) *We Are All in Shock: How Overwhelming Experiences Shatter You...And What You Can Do About It.* New Jersey: Career Press, Inc.

Mines, S. (2010) 'Special Needs Children 11 Elements of Integrative Bodywork.' *Massage & Bodywork September/October* 2010, 34-43.

Mines, S., Morris, T. and Persun, D. (2012) 'The Effect of Applied Touch on the Behavior of Autistic Children.' In Press.

Moburg, K.U. (2003) *The Oxytocin Factor: Tapping The Hormone Of Calm, Love, And Healing.* Massachusetts: Perseus Books Group. (Original work published in 2000).

Montgomery, S. and Grandin, T. (2012) *Temple Grandin: How the Girl Who Loved Cows Embraced Autism and Changed the World.* New York: Houghton Mifflin Harcourt Publishing Company.

Mooney, J. (2011) *Neurodiversity: A Compass to a Changing World.* YouTube: Conference on Inclusive Education. Accessed at http://www.youtube.com/watch?v=srWWMVKG56M.

Mooney, J. (2007) *The Short Bus A Journey Beyond Normal*. New York: Henry Holt and Company, LLC.

Natenshon, A.H. and Toomey, K. (2012) *Feeding Disorders and Picky Eating in Infants and Children,* Treating Eating Disorders.com.

L.N. (2012) Personal Testimony

ONE News (2011) *Software promises access for the blind and the deaf.* Source: ONE News. Accessed at http://tvnz.co.nz/technology-news/software-promises-access-blind-and-deaf-4666133

Perry, B., and Szalavitz, M. (2011) *Born For Love: Why Empathy is Essential – and Endangered.* New York: HarperCollins Publishers.

Porges, S.W. (2004) *The Vagus: A Mediator of Behavioral and Physiologic Features Associated with Autism.* Bauman, M. L. and Kemper, T. L. (eds), The Neurobiology of Autism. Baltimore: Johns Hopkins University Press.

Powers, R. (2005) *Mark Twain: A Life*. New York: Simon and Schuster, p. 8.

Prince-Hughes, D. (2004) *Songs of the Gorilla Nation: My Journey Through Autism.* New York: Crown Publishing Group, p. 31.

Rice, C. (2009, Original version published in 2006) 'Prevalence of Autism Spectrum Disorders and Developmental Disabilities.' *Morbidity and Mortality Weekly Report Surveillance Summaries* 58(SS10); 1-20.

Robison, J.E. (2007 & 2008) *Look Me in the Eye: My Life With Asperger's.* New York: Three Rivers Press.

Roelfsema, M.T., Hoekstra, R.A., Allison, C., Wheelwright, S., Brayne, C., et al (2012) *Are Autism Spectrum Conditions More Prevalent in an Information-Technology Region? A School-Based Study of Three Regions in the Netherlands.* Journal of Autism and Developmental Disorders, DOI: 10.1007/s10803-011-1302-1.

Schneider, M. (1998) Self-Healing: *My Life and Vision.* New York: Penguin.

Schneider, M. (2010) *Meir Schneider My Life And Vision.* YouTube: Interview by Iain McNay. Accessed at http://www.youtube.com/watch?v=OmwtKt5TwNs.

Science Daily (2010) *Childhood Stress Such as Abuse or Emotional Neglect Can Result in Structural Brian Changes,* Dublin: Trinity College.

Sensory Processing Disorder (2012). Accessed at http://www.sensory-processing-disorder.com/weighted-blankets.html

Shaywitz, S. E. (1996)'Dyslexia.' *Scientific American* November 1996.

Tammet, Daniel (2006) *Born On A Blue Day: Inside the Extraordinary Mind of an Autistic Savant.* New York: Free Press, a Division of Simon & Schuster, Inc.

Tammet, Daniel (2009) *Embracing the Wide Sky*: *A Tour Across the Horizons of the Mind.* New York: Free Press, a Division of Simon & Schuster, Inc.

Teresa, M. (2001, first published 1995) *No Greater Love*. California: New World Library, p. 94.

Tesla, N. and Hunt, S. (2011) *My Inventions and Other Writings*. New York: Penguin Classic.

The Center for AAC & Autism (2009). Accessed at http://www.aacandautism.com/why-aac.

Vonder Hulls, D. S., Walker, L. K., Powell, J. M. (2006) 'Clinicians' perceptions of the benefits of aquatic therapy for young children with autism: a preliminary study.' *Phys Occup Ther Pediatr.* 26, 1-2, 13-22.

Yeats, W.B. (2010, first published 1916) *Reveries Over Childhood and Youth*. London: Jessica Kingsley Publishers, p. 49.

Young, A. (2010) *Autism: From the Traditional Chinese Medicine Perspective*, Keefer Michael.

About the Author

Dr. Stephanie Mines is a psychologist whose unique understanding comes from her academic research as well as her extensive work in the field. Her stories of personal transformation have led many listeners to become deeply committed to the healing journey. Dr. Mines understands shock from every conceivable perspective. She has investigated it as a survivor, a professional, a healthcare provider, and as a trainer of staffs of institutions and agencies. Her blend of Western and Eastern modalities offers the best of both paradigms. She is devoted to ending the lineage of shock and trauma for individuals and the world.

Dr. Mines is the Program Director of the DOM Project, a non-profit organization dedicated to providing alternative health options for a broad spectrum of populations. As Director, she is responsible for disseminating information to communities in

Dr. Stephanie Mines

need, especially people suffering from illness that results from shock and trauma, survivors of domestic violence, families and children, and people living with neurodiversity including autism and other sensory integration challenges.

Dr. Mines' previous book, *We Are All in Shock: How Overwhelming Experiences Shatter You and What You Can Do About It,* (New Page Books, 2003), presents a comprehensive application of the healing system she has developed. Presently, she is working on a new book concerning the impact of war from the perspective of families and children who experience the effects of a returning veteran with PTSD or combat shock. The titles are still in process.